2/95

Albuquerque Academy
Library
6400 Wyoming Blvd. N.E.
Albuquerque, N.M. 87109

D1015139

SALVADOR'S
CHILDREN

A Sandstone Book

SALVADOR'S CHILDREN
A Song for Survival

Lea Marenn

Drawings by M. J. Marenn

A Helen Hooven Santmyer Prize Winner

Ohio State University Press
Columbus

The publication of this book was supported in part by a Seed Grant from the Office of Research at the Ohio State University.
Ohio Arts Council Individual Artist Fellowship Recipient, 1993

Copyright © 1993 by Lea Marenn.
All rights reserved.

Library of Congress Cataloging-in-Publication Data

Marenn, Lea.
   Salvador's children : a song for survival / Lea Marenn ; drawings by M.J. Marenn.
     p. cm.
   "A Sandstone book."
   ISBN 0–8142–0593–3 (cloth). — ISBN 0–8142–0594–1 (pbk.)
    1. Intercountry adoption—El Salvador—Personal narratives.
    2. Intercountry adoption—United States—Personal narratives.
    3. Children, Adopted—El Salvador—Personal narratives.
    4. Children—El Salvador—Social conditions. I. Title.
HV875.58.S2M37 1993
362.7'34—dc20
                                   92–593
                                     CIP

Text and jacket design by Donna Hartwick.
Type set in Baskerville and Bernhard by The Composing Room of Michigan, Inc., Grand Rapids, MI.
Printed by Braun-Brumfield, Ann Arbor, MI.

The paper in this book meets the guidelines for permanence and durability of the Committee on Production Guidelines for Book Longevity of the Council on Library Resources. ∞

9 8 7 6 5 4 3 2 1

362.734
MAR
1993

. . . the gray orphans
the volcano spitting bright lava
and the dead guerrillero
and the thousand betrayed faces,
the children who are watching
so they can tell of it.

Claribel Alegría,
Flowers from the Volcano

ELEGY

My relatives are the dead.
They are: Cándida and Felipe
Cándida and Felipe's children: Victór and Rosa
(their names are known)
Cándida and Felipe's two grandchildren: children of Marta
Cándida and Felipe's son-in-law: husband of Marta
Cándida and Felipe's brother-in-law: husband of Pilar
Cándida's father and mother
Cándida's two younger brothers: the twins
Cándida's three sisters, two brothers-in-law, and their children
(their names are unknown).

My relatives are the missing.
They are: Felipe's father and mother, José and Antonia
Felipe's elder brother Pablo, his wife and three children
Felipe's elder sister Olivia and her four children
Felipe's younger sister Pilar and her four children
Cándida and Felipe's eldest daughter, Marta
Cándida and Felipe's grandchild Marinita, daughter of Marta
Cándida and Felipe's eldest son, Miguel.

My relatives are the survivors.
They are: Cándida and Felipe's third son, Aurelio
Cándida and Felipe's fourth son, Ramón
Cándida and Felipe's youngest daughter, María de Jesús.

I live in the house of the survivors
I live in the house of the missing
I live in the house of the dead.

PART

1

YANKEE ITINERARY

Cándida. **For all the brush and the trees you might** *not have noticed the orange ball slip its layers of fat over the edge of the world. Oh, the mind spins, remembering the tamarindos, the morning sun, the cool shade in the back of the house in the late afternoon. But you knew well the sharp cut of the mountainside, and so it was dark of a sudden as you finished serving the beans and tortillas. Then you must have crossed the yellow-brown earth, heard the scraping sound of your bare feet this way and that, between and among all the others. At that time of year it was too early to lie down, and the fire was good, keeping the chill off for a while, and some of the dreams. Your wide moon face must have been black in the dark as you turned from the fire. Then you became the flicker of your eyes as you moved them back and forth, and the bones under the shadows of your cheeks.*

This was Chinchontepec—there were no more roses on the volcano. Oh, toward the noon hour it was hot. Each day you met the sun and the sweat, and someone was in the next row, and in the next. Your arms and backs ached, there was no reason for talk. Your eyes and your machetes could split a sugarcane stalk in two, but you bent your backs and cut the stalks down; sorted them and stacked them up, one after the other. When it was time you would know what to do. You knew it in your backs and in your shoulder blades. You felt the earth firm under your feet. You would not feel dizzy from the sun, nor from fear. Who didn't feel fear? Who didn't know that all you had was your machetes and your eyes and your sweat? The owners had the land and hired the foremen. The army had the guns, and at

3

night they crept disguised into villages and left bru-
talized bodies behind. If the volcano erupted in cross-
fire, who would be the victims?

　　When there is a matanza no one forgets, not even
the dead. Not even Aquino's dried-up Pipil head, caged
on a hill for 150 years near the capital of your prov-
ince. San Vincente—it's where you went to the market
each week. Day after day, you stared into the distance
and saw that the land boiled in the sun. But you knew
that you had hundreds of years of the fires up and down
this road, on this and on the other hillsides to the north,
east, and west. You knew there were families and clans
and villages of fires all around. You knew well the se-
cret pathways into the lost green of the mountains, and
the gray webs of tunnels lining the insides of the
volcano.

　　Chinchontepec. Each day you walked on the long
road and looked at the horizon forever. And the stones
recorded for all time the tracks you beat with your feet.
The stones on that road would not grow—they stayed
the same size and shape.

It was the state orphanage for girls and young children, Rosa Virginia, right next to the Ilopango women's prison. A guard at the top of the drive signaled to us to stop, then stepped to the car to check our papers. As we waited for him to unlock the gate, I took a postage-stamp-sized snapshot out of my purse and looked one last time at the black-and-white I.D. photograph of a girl that a clerk at the court of minors had handed me earlier that morning. A mug shot, I thought to myself, attempting to discern the tense, withholding gesture of the body. Wise, somber, warm, scared—the child's eyes seemed to pierce the lens of the camera. Who was she? Where was she from? Did she really have no one left? What right did I have to decide her future for her? Then my mind went blank, as it had each time I had asked myself these questions over the past weeks, and my eyes rested on the angle between the girl's straight shoulder and her short tousled hair.

All I knew was her age and her name—María de Jesús, age eight. Less than three weeks earlier, at the end of February 1984, I had received a telephone call from the woman in the adoptive parent organization responsible for El Salvador: "I have

5

good news—we have a child for you. Her name is María de Jesús. She is eight years old, and she is healthy and normal by El Salvador standards. All her paperwork is ready. There is no birth certificate to be found, but she is probably an orphan. Incidentally, María de Jesús has two younger brothers who are being adopted by Ralph and Doris Novak—a couple from Pittsburgh. If you agree, it would be best if you and they traveled together before the Salvadoran elections at the end of next month. Of course, you'll have to come up here for one last orientation meeting."

"Oh yes!" I said. "María de Jesús? How wonderful! Her name is María de Jesús and she's eight years old. Wonderful! Yes! Yes! I can be ready to go as soon as I get a flight." Elated after months of uncertain anticipation, María de Jesús' new adoptive mother, age forty, healthy and normal by North American standards, said yes.

Five adolescent girls came running toward our car as we turned the corner at the bottom of the drive into the empty courtyard of Rosa Virginia. "¡La gringa! ¡La gringa! Give me, give me. Take me, take me, take me!" they giggled and hummed and pleaded as we opened the doors of the car to get out. One of the girls had only one arm. Another girl's hair was a dull orange color and stood straight up from her scalp. Smiling at the girls, using sign language and blurting out unconnected Spanish words, I tried to follow the interpreter and the Novaks to the door of the orphanage. The girls quickly surrounded me, pulling on my arms, patting my hair, stroking my dress. Surely they knew that they were considered too old to be adopted. One of the girls put her head on my breast. I hugged her, then broke away.

Inside, we were told to wait in the foyer. Remarkably, it was dark and cool. While our interpreter went over papers with the director of the orphanage, Doris and Ralph Novak and I stood awkwardly in the small foyer, waiting to meet our soon-to-be children. On the plane and in the hotel the night before we had talked excitedly about our common interests and emotions, but now we were too nervous for conversation, restricting ourselves to occasional comments about the condition of our sweaty clothes and the heat outside.

Only a week ago we had never heard of each other, and now we were relatives of a sort. Ralph was an auto mechanic, and Doris had just quit her secretarial job to become a full-time housekeeper and mother. I was an academic about to join the swelling ranks of single working mothers. None of us could imagine how our lives would change from this moment—we lived in the urgency of the present.

Before long, two matrons brought in a girl and a little boy to meet us—María de Jesús and her brother Ramón. The children stood rigid and silent, their eyes cast downward, their feet together. I felt the heat rush to my temples and my hands begin to shake as I stepped toward the girl. I squatted down in front of her and caught her eye.

I know that, from the very first moment I saw my daughter María, I loved her. As I squatted in front of her and looked into her eyes, I wondered why I hadn't wanted to have a child years earlier. Then I mumbled something I had vaguely rehearsed in Spanish. I don't remember the words I used, but I told her in a voice I now know was hoarse that I hoped she would accept me; that I would love her, take care of her, and be her new mother.

Standing straight and rigid in front of me, clutching a doll and casting her frightened eyes to the ground, she seemed so frail. I was the tall, blonde woman from the north bearing gifts—la gringa. By squatting and saying a few phrases in broken Spanish, I must have wanted to unload before her the burden of my colonial inheritance, five centuries of European and American injustices—my guilt. Miraculously, the load seemed to vanish, and there was nothing between us but our separate wounds and our fear of each other.

Several months later, back in the States, I mustered up the courage to ask María what she had felt at the time. She told me she had known nothing about the adoption until a few minutes before she was brought out to meet me. "Hurry," the nurse Luisa had said, out of breath, when she found María in her building doing her chores. "Quick, wash your face and put on this dress. The gringos are here and you're being adopted. You can take one toy with you."

María did not hesitate for a moment and did as she was told. She took Rosita, a white-skinned doll with platinum hair, donated to the orphanage by other gringos a few months earlier. Then she saw me in the foyer—trembling, as she liked to put it afterward, in my white blouse, navy blue suit, and red-and-white spectator shoes. I must have appeared alien to her, wrapped in—of all things—the colors of the American flag. And what did María remember of the scene as she sat among her toys in her North American bedroom? For her, there seemed to have been little pathos. "Mamá!" she shrieked gleefully. "¡Mamá! ¡Qué cómica estabas! ¡Tú temblabas!"

María had been a mother to Ramón for over a year, begging in the streets for food, trying to keep him clean, battling the parasites that caused him pain and bloated his belly. He stood close to her that day, already dressed in the brand new green-and-orange sports shirt and shorts Ralph and Doris Novak had brought for him from Pittsburgh. One hand held fast to María's; with the other he accepted a small teddy bear from his new adoptive parents. The Novaks smiled through their tears of joy at the little boy as they spoke to him in elementary English with some familiar Italian and Spanish phrases thrown in. Neither of the children said a word to each other or anyone else, but kept heads bowed and stared at the stone floor.

Less than ten minutes after this first meeting, we were escorted by the matrons to the car waiting outside. Apparently it was a standard transaction. I was overwhelmed by conflicting emotions, but determined to carry out what I had come to do. Still, I wanted to postpone the extraordinary separation— an entire culture and history turned on this moment. "Does María have a special friend?" I asked the director of the orphanage as the interpreter opened the car door on the driver's side. She smiled politely at me, then turned to one of the girls crowding around us and called out a name.

A girl in a worn, but not shabby, pale blue dress, Melva, stepped toward María and put her hand carefully on her shoulder, while María, dressed in a similarly worn, hand-me-down pink dress—clearly from previous gringos—remained perfectly stoic, her eyes lowered, her feet at attention, her doll held at her waist. The pain I refused to acknowledge was so great that I stepped back and began to snap pictures. During the shuffling and the picture taking, neither of the girls said a word, except that as we stepped to the car, Melva grabbed María and whispered in her ear. A year later María confided those words to me: "No te vayas a olvidar de mí." Don't you forget me.

I reeled from the scene. Through the dust rising at our feet I saw another courtyard, another waiting car, another awkward parting. It was the year 1949, a European summer. In the middle of a farmyard, an American G.I. leaned against an army Jeep and casually smoked a cigarette, waiting to transport his passengers—a man, a woman, and a six-year-old girl—to a displaced persons' camp in Munich. The man and the woman said their final good-byes to an old farmer and his family gathered on the doorstep. Then they walked

toward the car and waited, while the little girl cried as she had
never cried before, clinging desperately to the skirts of the
old farm woman who tried to console her. It was no use. Finally the child had to be ripped from the old woman, and the
Jeep started quickly and sped away.

Behind that scene stood a jumble of images from the end
of the Second World War in Central Europe. Hurried, jerky
flights down stairs into a cellar bomb shelter in the middle of
the night; a baby in her mother's arms, the air-raid siren
screaming in her ears from across the street. A small room
with a makeshift crib; a man in a military uniform waving a
revolver in front of a crying child, threatening to shoot. Collapsed buildings, an apartment without an exterior wall,
bodies in the rubble. A train journey with armed soldiers who
had shiny metal guns and wore thick, shiny boots; the run for
a small woods, a mother throwing herself on her child, planes
screaming in strafing formation. People crowding the high-
ways, carrying bundles, pulling carts loaded with suitcases,
pushing children and old people in baby carriages. Horse-
drawn wagons and army deserters, tired bodies collapsing at
the side of the road next to the dying and the dead. Finally, in
a village farmyard in April 1945, where tank tracks were still
fresh from a brief occupation by a retreating company of
storm troops, an old farmer and his wife offered a two-year-
old girl a small beige pillow and a glass of milk.

Quickly, a last memory followed. It was the spring of
1952. A nine-year old girl in a town in upstate New York
raced with her classmates down Ontario Street to Western Avenue, where a parade was rumored to be coming from the
armory. When they arrived, breathless, sure enough, for as
far as one could see either way, army-green tanks, Jeeps, and
transport vehicles filled with soldiers crept down the treelined avenue. The girl was caught up in the excitement of the
crowd, but all at once she felt a sharp pain in her chest, and

then, right after that, a big clap, as though an iron door had swung open, then suddenly locked inside her. She stood transfixed, numb with fear but not knowing why, remembering the pain but not the feeling of it. She knew she had been in the presence of these soldiers and vehicles before, but from that day onward the person who remembered what it felt like was locked behind a door. She stood wavering on the curb—part of her wanting to be carefree with the other children, the other part fearful, feeling something was different and very wrong with her. The third person—the little girl who knew the source of her pain—had disappeared. After a while the nine-year-old mumbled good-bye and something about tomorrow to her schoolmates, then walked away alone, trying to gain control of the confusion that was starting to envelop her. When she arrived home she didn't say a word about the incident to her parents, and thereafter avoided listening to old stories about the war. She was going to be an American girl.

We were leaving the state orphanage for girls and young children, Rosa Virginia, right next to the Ilopango women's prison. At the top of the drive the car stopped, and we waited for the guard to open the gate. Tightening my grip on María, who was sitting on my lap, I turned around to look back for a last time. The pink-hued cobblestone driveway was flanked on the right, the highway side, by a twenty-foot wooden fence. On the left, a twenty-foot steel fence with barbed wire on top separated us from the grounds of the women's prison. A huge tree on the prison grounds pushed its flurry of pink blossoms over the wall toward the opposite fence. Beyond the pink blossoms, toward the orphanage at the bottom of the drive, voluptuous green trees arched toward the sky. On dark Ilopango nights, I thought to myself, the women must whisper secrets and crawl over the prison wall to visit with their children.

CHAPTER

2

Every time we went around a curve I could feel the flesh of our legs—wet, like gelatin, slipping and sliding against each other. We were en route to the state boys' orphanage to pick up María and Ramón's brother Aurelio. It was an uneasy balancing act, yet María's face revealed nothing. She kept her shoulders stiff, her knees tight, her ankles pinned together as she sat on my lap in the passenger seat of the car. Vera Bock, the young interpreter next to us, tried to make conversation with her for the first fifteen minutes, translating for me. María responded to her questions only once, proudly asserting her name: María de

Jesús Remas Ramírez. Her voice was barely audible, but her words cut the air like a razor. With that she was finished, and Vera eventually gave up. In the back seat, stuffing raisins into his mouth, Ramón sat smiling dreamily between his new adoptive parents.

It was almost midday, sticky and hot, and the sun's rays were ruthless. On my left was María's frightened, immobile face, glued with sweat to my cheek. On my right passed the weary, anxious faces of the citizens of San Salvador. Drivers honked their horns, cars stopped and started abruptly, and faded blue-brown human throngs spilled onto the sidewalks. Lines formed on the street corners while women hastily grilled food on open stoves. Their children, barefoot and playing with makeshift toys, sat on the pavement or in the dirt at their feet.

Overwhelmed by the multitude of foreign images, I turned to our interpreter, Vera—who with her fair skin, blonde hair, and blue eyes looked more like me than anyone I had yet seen in El Salvador—and complimented her on her English. My opening managed to break the deadly silence of the front seat.

"Oh it's so funny, everybody says that," she chirped, obviously delighted to make conversation. "But you are the first one who says my English sounds European. Yes, I was born here, but my father is European. We used to travel as a family every summer, and my sisters and brother and I went to schools here and there. Yes, I also speak German and French. At the bank I work for my father and take care of the international correspondence."

Vera's polite chatter put me at ease. She could have been one of my students, finishing college late or working toward an advanced degree. I saw women like her every day—smart, scared, vulnerable. They worked hard, and one wanted to support and protect them. I asked Vera how she liked her work.

"Oh yes, I like very much being a working woman. Most women my age are married and raising children, but I don't want to be in a hurry. Do you know the word machismo? That influence is very strong here, but in our generation some of us women do not accept that. We feel we should have more choices, more freedoms. Don't you think it is important, too, for women to be self-supporting and independent?"

Yes, of course, I agreed. High up in the air, a political billboard with the bright blue, red, and white colors of the fascist

Arena Party dominated the skyline. "Who do you think will win the election?" I asked Vera, pleased that we had so quickly established a rapport.

"Oh, what a mess," she rejoined with a high lilt. "It's really not dangerous for Americans here, so don't worry. But I tell you, the left is causing so much trouble right now. You know, the muchachos—we call them the boys. Now, just two weeks before the elections, they think they can trick us because the international press is here. Do you remember the gasoline station we passed near the Presidente?"

Yes, I nodded. I remembered it, a familiar Texaco or Shell station.

"Well, they bombed it last week. No one was hurt, but still it's blatant terrorism—don't you agree?"

Yes, of course, I nodded again. It didn't matter, as Vera hardly paused for a breath.

"It is an outrage! We never know when the muchachos will surprise us again. They only cause trouble! It was so nice in our country, but in the last years even your congressmen and senators think they can get involved in our affairs. I am sorry to tell you this, but your Congress is terribly naive. They believe anything the liberals say. They say everything is about human rights, and now the Americans are even telling us how to hold our elections. You know, our President Duarte is a man without a spine, a puppet of your naive liberals in your Congress. He goes to Washington to ask for aid, and they tell him what he first has to do in his own country. Really, he is only a friend of the left. It is a disgrace, I tell you! Maybe he and your liberal congressmen would prefer to live in Cuba!"

I straightened up and tightened my hold on María, who had slid down my lap from the sweat. She was engrossed in the contents of the pink unicorn purse I had brought for her—a short pink pencil, a tiny heart-shaped pad of paper, a

Mickey Mouse eraser, a yellow sequined comb, Cabbage Patch stickers, a few pieces of gum and candy. Sketching for María a flower with big petals and leaves on a pink heart-shaped piece of paper, I asked Vera if she seriously preferred the Arena Party and its leader Roberto d'Aubuisson, who was known, after all, to be directly involved in political murders and the right-wing death squads.

"I tell you honestly," she lowered her voice just a bit, "d'Aubuisson is the only person who can keep our country from falling apart. Well, I admit his Arena Party is a bit extreme, they do silly things. Once they are in power, of course, those extremes will not need to continue. You know, our best people support Arena. The accusations of your members of Congress against them are absolutely false. Believe me, Arena is the only party that can get our economy on its feet again, and d'Aubuisson is the one person who will finally deal with the left, get rid of them once and for all. Believe me, the opposition is made up of criminals—dangerous criminals, every one of them."

I was stunned by Vera's diatribe. What kind of politics did a fairly personable, educated woman have who espoused the fascist Arena Party and a reputed killer like Roberto d'Aubuisson? A year after my trip I met a Salvadoran woman in political exile who had attended a private finishing school with Vera. "She is wealthy," my acquaintance said in a tone of understatement. "She belongs to one of the wealthiest families in El Salvador."

Vera was our official interpreter and guide in this country. She knew how to make international connections and to maneuver her way through the official channels of adoption in El Salvador. She knew how to communicate in Spanish with a frightened eight-year-old, and explain to her that I was her new mother. Whatever my opinions, I couldn't afford to quibble with Vera. She was my only proven link, my lifeline to the Salvadoran court system, the orphanage, the American embassy, and my daughter.

I looked down at María's sweaty head; wisps of her short hair were pasted to her forehead and around her ears. Still absorbed by the contents of the pink unicorn purse and examining each item with meticulous care, she had retreated fully into her silence. Her silence—what did it conceal? For the first time, I understood that I was no longer a mere observer of events in Central America. I had become a part of this American voyage from the north to the center, never to disengage again.

CHAPTER

3

The car pulled up to the curb in front of the state boys' orphanage. In less than five minutes María and Ramón's brother Aurelio, in a white shirt and pants cut off at the knee, was brought out to stand before us at the top of the steps. He had lost both his front teeth, and in a fearful, somewhat defiant gesture, held his fist in front of his mouth. Aurelio was only a head taller than Ramón, but his eyes told me that he was decades older—too old for six years.

The formalities were over. I was already at the bottom of the steps with Aurelio's sister and brother, holding María's hand while she watched Ra-

món eat a second box of raisins. Not one of the three children had yet openly acknowledged or said a word to another. Then I looked back and noticed that Aurelio was still at the top of the steps, fist in front of his mouth, eyes to the ground, struggling not to cry. Behind him, twelve- to fourteen-year-old boys stood at a distance, leaning awkwardly against the thick exterior wall of the building, and watched the scene with folded arms.

Ralph and Doris tried to comfort Aurelio. "We're your new parents, we love you," Ralph said to him through the interpreter, but it was the sound of his voice that mattered. Several orphanage workers crowded nervously around Aurelio and urged him to walk down the stairs. "It is not so unusual for the children to be frightened," they assured the Novaks. "He is only frightened," they repeated one by one in halting English, while each of them appeared to be whispering something encouraging in Aurelio's ear.

It was clear that there was a special reason for Aurelio's suffering. He appeared to be waiting for somebody, something. The tears had begun to trickle down his cheeks, and he used the back of his clenched hand to wipe them. There was some good reason why he didn't want to go, but the orphanage staff was silent, and no one else knew what to do. I asked Vera several times to inquire about the problem, but each time she smiled and replied that he was "only frightened" and this was normal. Standing straight and never looking up, Aurelio continued to wipe his tears with his fist. The boys leaning against the wall behind him watched the scene. They, too, were silent.

We could have forced Aurelio down the stairs and dragged him into the car, and in the long run that might have been the best option, but it would have remained imprinted on his mind forever. Or he could have stayed at the orphanage, not to be exposed to yet another loss, another departure, another extreme change. The next station for the older boys in the orphanage was inevitably the army. While the first alternative appeared cruel, the second seemed irresponsible at this point.

Suddenly, I had an idea. It would implicate me forever in this colonial history of North-South rationalizations and exchanges. I took María and Ramón and walked toward Vera, who was standing alone, poised but at a loss. "Vera," I said in a tone of authority, "tell María to take Ramón with her and go to Aurelio. Tell her to tell him they are going to the United

States to live with new parents who will care for them and love them. They will have clothes, a nice house, and food. Tell her to tell him that he will be living together with Ramón and that she will be close by. Tell her to take his hand and lead him down the steps to the car. Tell her he must leave. Tell her it is better for him, for all three of them, this way."

Vera leaned down toward María, and in her kittenish voice she relayed the message in Spanish. Keeping her eyes fixed all the while on mine, María listened carefully until Vera was finished. She hesitated only for a moment. She said nothing—she knew what to do. She turned to Ramón, took his hand, walked with him up the steps, and stopped in front of Aurelio. They looked at each other, said not one word. Then María took Aurelio's hand—on the other side she still had Ramón. She took one step down with Ramón. Aurelio followed. Slowly, the three of them walked down the steps, one a head taller than the other, each probably separated eighteen months from the next. "Ramón and I have lighter, smoother hair, more like our mother," María told me much later. "Aurelio looks more like our father."

By the time the children reached the bottom of the steps, Ralph and Doris had joined them and were patting Aurelio on the shoulder. Vera, a smile of victory on her face, was busy opening the doors of the car and hurrying the children—we still had two appointments to keep. The director and the social workers waved good-bye to us reassuringly.

For a moment, I stood alone at the bottom of the steps and turned to look up at the adolescent boys who still watched the scene, leaning awkwardly, tentatively, against the orphanage wall. Now we were the ones who would never forget.

ALBUQUERQUE ACADEMY
LIBRARY

"I promise you, after this we have only one last stop!" Vera joked as she pulled into the parking space in front of a two-story medical office building. Exhausted, three adults and three children climbed out of the car and followed Vera up the stairs single file to the doctor's office on the second floor.

The physician, dressed in his white coat, his stethoscope around his neck, received us in a white room with a white cot and stainless steel utensils. I didn't know how many doctors María had seen, but it appeared that Vera was experienced in bringing orphaned children and their new adoptive parents to him. She di-

rected her toward the cot, telling her not to be shy and to take off her clothes, while the doctor silently scrutinized María from across the room. When he finally began to examine her—Vera all the while telling her when and how to move, and that the doctor would not hurt her— he kept himself as far as possible from the cot, only his hands at the end of his outstretched arms doing the work of gnawing at her abdomen and her back. When he was finished and had left the room—he had not yet said a word—María hunched her shoulders over her bare chest and wrapped her arms around her exposed abdomen. Vera told her in her gayest voice that she should get dressed. María turned away from us both to do this. Instinctively, I turned to face another wall, embarrassed for us all.

"All the girls had to be examined by a doctor when they first came to the orfanato, just in case," María told me months later. "There was a little girl, maybe five years old, and before she came to the orfanato she was hurt by a man. She had to walk with her legs way open—it was hard for her to walk. The children teased her because it looked funny. But really she couldn't help it, it hurt her. Slowly it got better and she walked almost like everybody else. I remember she was adopted a little time before me. Maybe now she is in Estados Unidos, too."

Sitting with María and Vera in the doctor's office in front of his desk, I had no trouble understanding what the doctor was saying: María was a healthy girl and there was absolutely nothing wrong with her. Then he stood up, reached over to pat her on the shoulder with the index and middle fingers of his left hand, and signaled with a nod of his head that we could leave. I paid the bill to the secretary in the next room.

Next, at the photographer's shop down the street, Aurelio and Ramón took their places one after the other on the tall stool. It was fun to have pictures snapped by a man who made strange faces, said silly things, and handed you a color image of yourself.

Now it was María's turn. Having entrusted the doll Rosita and her pink unicorn purse to me, she walked deliberately to the stool in front of the magic box. Then she positioned herself carefully on the stool, brushed her skirt down with her hands, folded them in her lap, straightened her back, and let her legs hang motionless. Her face shone from the sweat, and she waited with hardly a breath as the photographer prepared the camera. Quickly, at the last minute, I ran to adjust her new pink barrette. María liked the barrette, and the attention. A split second later, I jumped behind the photographer and gesticulated wildly, making my face like a baboon's.

The shutter clicked, everybody sighed. María glided from the stool and came to reclaim her purse and Rosita. In only a few minutes, the photographer returned with the prize: a visa photo—the first picture María had ever seen of herself. It showed a three-quarter face, the barrette firmly in place, the left ear exposed, the eyelids heavy, the eyes mellow, the cheeks flushed and rounded. Her lips were closed, but pulled back in a wide grin.

5

The late-afternoon rays of the sun were long, the shadows of the evening private. María and I had completed our first day together. After we arrived at the hotel I had helped María bathe and dress, and ordered food to be brought up to our room. We had taken a long time to eat, to use sign language, to giggle and blush, and to try out foreign-sounding words. We had taken pictures of María sitting on the hotel room's terrace in her new pink dress, showing off her painted fingernails. We had cut out dresses and pants for Ramona, the paper doll, and used brand-new crayons to color in two coloring books.

It was bedtime. Aurelio and Ramón had gone into the next room with the Novaks, and María and I sat side by side on her bed, looking at pictures of a blonde American girl and a lamb in a book called *El corderito.* I stumbled through the Spanish words on each page, but María was patient with me and pointed now and then to a detail in the pictures. I was the blonde American girl, she was the lamb. When I was finished, she wanted me to read the book to her again. No one had ever read to her before; no one had ever put a book of pictures and printed pages in her hand. I knew that I would read *El corderito* to her again and again, that we would sit like this, night after night, our backs against the wall and our legs outstretched, reading books and looking at pictures. I was the blonde American girl, she was the lamb.

It was time to go to sleep. María walked in her new night-gown to the bed still covered with books, crayons, paper-doll clothes, pink unicorn purse, the brown-skinned doll Jennie I had brought from the States, and white-skinned Rosita with platinum hair from the orphanage. In a flash, María gath-ered up all these items, ordered them, and placed them with the greatest reverence on the floor next to the bed. Rosita and her North American sister Jennie sat with their backs to the wall. The other objects, carefully stacked, lay at their feet.

Then María turned to the bed, folded back the covers, and adjusted the pillow. A split second later she was sitting upright on the bed, her legs straight and as close together as possible between the sheets, her toes pointing under the top sheet and the blanket at the ceiling. She stretched her upper body toward her toes, patted the blanket around her feet, an-kles, calves, knees, thighs, hips. Then she lay down flat, con-tinued patting and brought the blanket skintight to her waist and ribs, then tucked it under her arms. With her head low on the pillow, she stretched both arms behind her and stared at the ceiling. I felt superfluous during this silent bedtime ritual—she clearly expected no help from me.

For several months María continued to prepare her be-longings, her body, and her bed this way each night. I had learned from one of the nurses at the orphanage that of all the hundreds of girls, María was the most particular, the cleanest, the neatest. Tears streamed down the nurse's face as she described how María went each day to Ramón's building after her chores. Every day she inspected his body to make sure he was clean, healthy, and dressed. Every day she sat and played with him. "I have never encountered such a child," cried the nurse. "You must talk, talk, talk to her. Hable! Hable!" she cried, as we began walking away. "You must help her to talk. Talk to her, talk. She is the most shy, the most quiet."

Why? Vera translated only a word here and there as she hurried me to the car. Finally, when we were out of the nurse's sight, she quickly turned to me and said, "No one knows why. She is just a sweet little shy girl. Be patient and talk to her. Look how adorable she is, and so pretty. You can see how everyone in the orphanage loves her. There is no problem—she is just very shy."

The deep, hollow eyes of the Salvadoran children who stare into the eternity and finality of the moment—María. What about her mother and father? Where were her grandparents, and her aunts and uncles? What happened to them that she felt so alone—unable to speak, unable to sleep, unable to dream? What was she thinking as she stared at the blank white ceiling? What did she see, or want to see? Was there room on the ceiling for me?

The adoption papers from the court said only that she was an orphan, and no one had come in a year to claim her. Any further questions were met by smiles, and silence. "I don't think anybody knew how to find us," María told me much later. "We just knew our life in our houses up there in San Antonio, and that's what we liked. Anyway, it was too far and it was too dangerous. People could see we were poor. They don't like the poor people when we try to do very much. They shoot you when you do much. I didn't believe anybody from my family would find me in the orphanage, and it was true."

"María, quieres Rosita?" I said, and held the doll out to her, suggesting she could have her while she slept. She gazed at me for half a minute, then gestured with her eyes toward the items on the floor. Rosita had to wait until tomorrow; at night her place was on the floor, next to the bed.

María closed her eyes. Her arms extended behind her head, her legs were straight together, her toes pointed upward; the blanket was molded to her body like a glove. The only sign of life was her breathing, ever so slight, yet regular. Carefully, I put Rosita down next to brown-skinned Jennie, her North American sister.

Outside our hotel room was a tropical garden of green lawn and red-orange flowers. I stepped from the tiled floor of the room to the concrete of the terrace, from the terrace to the lawn. The air was moist and still. A bird called with a parrot-like sound as I listened to the crickets everyone heard in El Salvador that night. Somewhere in the province of San Vicente, or Chalatenango, or San Miguel, Salvadoran peasants were spending their last night alive. Over fifty thousand of them had been killed in the last five years. Of their grandparents' generation, twenty thousand were killed in the year 1932 alone. La matanza—the massacre. Everyone in El Salvador knew what that meant. When there was a matanza, no one forgot it, not even the dead.

That night, twenty, forty, or hundreds of Salvadoran peasants were the army's dead of tomorrow. It was 9 P.M. They must have been tired, stroking their children's foreheads for the last time. Or their bodies were entwined in love, glistening, satisfied. Perhaps they had argued, or they were looking quietly out of their huts at the stars, hearing the chorus of crickets, dreaming of death—for the last time.

A lean figure emerged from the other side of the garden. It was the hotel guard, a rifle slung over his shoulder. He smiled at me quizzically. I had seen him earlier as he made his rounds and nodded my way. Now he had heard my door slide

open and saw me walking outside. He was doing his job—
probably it didn't pay much, just enough. Better for a woman
alone to be inside at night, he gestured. Adjusting his rifle on
his shoulder, he saluted politely and walked away.

As I slipped silently around the room, turning off lights,
preparing for bed, I could see drops of perspiration begin to
form on María's forehead. When my back was turned, I could
feel her eyes watching me, tracking my every move. Every
time I turned to look at her, there were larger bubbles of perspiration on her forehead; more terror, more fear. She was
breathing regularly, but ever so lightly. Her eyes were closed,
yet she was awake. María didn't know tears anymore. The
bubbles of perspiration turned into lakes of sweat, flooding
the pillow.

My place was between the lines—between the walls of the
room, the objects on the floor, and María. I put a cool, damp
washcloth on her forehead, and she let me wipe her wet scalp
and neck with a towel. "May I lie down on this bed, too," I
whispered in broken Spanish, "between you and the dolls on
the floor?" She looked at me for a long time. Then, slowly, she
nodded. I lay down and heard her breathing deepen as the
minutes passed. Finally, she was asleep.

I turned off the last light and went to the other bed. My
shell had cracked, and I was heavy. My bed was wide and soft,
and I was heavy. I had given myself to this night, I couldn't
turn back. Gunshots? No, firecrackers splintered the sky in
the distance. A small bird cheeped in the tree at the window. I
inhaled the night air; the sliding terrace door was unlocked,
open. I smelled the earth, a heavy mixture of fallen flowers
and bones. I turned onto my right side with a groan. The
white sheet rustled. The grains of wood, the small glass panel
were above us. Yes, I knew where I was. I was in the grave. I
saw her face to face. Her eyes were open; she didn't smile, she

didn't frown. She remembered everything. I knew that she would take care of us. I recognized her: She was María's mother.

The air smelled rich and clear when I woke up in the morning. I was lying on my right side, still in my blue suit and my red-and-white spectator shoes, holding the washcloth and the towel. Through the open terrace door the morning light flooded the room. The sky was a brilliant blue, and the red-orange flowers raised their crowns to the sun. I looked over to María's bed. She was asleep—still on her back, her hands stretched behind her head, her legs together, her toes pointing at the ceiling. She had not moved an inch, but her breathing was regular and deep. The bubbles, the lakes of sweat, had dried.

CHAPTER

6

Grinning, María turned her head back toward Aurelio and squealed. Aurelio took the signal and dove forward in the water. She dove forward three feet ahead of him, and the chase was on. Around and around in the water they splashed and swam, diving like little dolphins, coming up for air, squealing, diving again, kicking, chasing each other around and around. Again María gave the signal with a quick turn of her head. Aurelio instantly leapt forward, diving, grabbing at her heels. She was too fast for him, but he was fast enough to keep her kicking, squealing, and beating the water like mad with her arms.

Ramón sat at the edge of the pool, stuffing crackers into his mouth. The crumbs fell on his bare limbs and his bloated belly. He didn't let his feet dangle in the water, and he hardly looked at his sister and brother playing in the children's pool. Ramón didn't know play, only hunger.

"Where did you learn to swim like that? ¿Nadar? ¿Dónde?" I asked in utter astonishment when the children came out of the water. Giggling and shivering as we wrapped them in the white hotel towels, they no longer exchanged a word or a glance. For a moment, everything threatened to become silent again.

"¡En la piscina!" María

29

suddenly blurted out, pointing to the huge adult swimming pool beyond us, empty except for a swimming instructor and a small group of young children at the shallow end, their mothers and a few hotel guests sipping cold drinks in lounge chairs at the edge of the pool. "¡En la piscina!" she cried again, much louder this time, pointing again to the adult pool, and with that, she and Aurelio surrendered themselves to uncontrollable giggling and laughter.

"Who taught you to swim like that? ¿Nadar? ¿De quién?" I asked the children again, aware for the first time that I had not dared to bring up the subject of their past until now. "De mi hermano," said Aurelio proudly, remembering for the first time in over an hour to cover his missing front teeth with his fist. "Si, de nuestro hermano, de Miguel," said María, her eyes bright and smiling.

"Your brother!" I gasped, understanding for the first time that the Novaks and I were not alone with the children. "I didn't know you had a brother! Where is he? ¿Dónde está? ¿Sabes tú? ¿Donde está? Tell us, where is your brother?"

The children stood rigid and silent, as if an umbrella of lead had suddenly stretched over their heads. Embarrassed, confused, and angry at me for bringing up the taboo subject, the Novaks gathered up their snacks, pop, and swim gear from the poolside table, muttered that they had had much too much sun, and hurried the boys to their room.

María and I sat down. Her expression was sullen, exhibiting the withholding gesture of anger and fear that I had first seen on the black-and-white identification photo presented to me the day before by the court of minors. "María, I want to help you. ¿Dónde está tu hermano?" I asked again. "Please tell me about your brother. Where is he? What happened to him?"

No. She didn't know. She shut down. No. She shrugged

her shoulders and frowned, staring at the box of paper dolls she had cheerfully packed up in the hotel room two hours earlier. After a few minutes she opened the box and started cutting out paper clothes. Slowly, carefully—every curve, every corner was perfect. We were silent. I reached across the table and picked up a second pair of scissors, and for the next hour we cut out clothes for an eight-year-old freckle-faced cardboard girl named Ramona.

Much later in the States, María drew a picture of three rectangular swimming pools on the outskirts of the provincial capital San Vicente, and told me the story.

"Some of the times our brother take us with his friends to the pools. It was so fun! Miguel throw us in the air and we splashed down in the water. He taught us to hold our nose and to dive, because he could do everything—swim, dive, jump, go upside down. Anyway, it was after we leave San Antonio and go down to San Vicente. There was much fighting all around us, and I think my father already died.

"Here, I show you on the paper—you see, the big blue blocks are the pools. And here we crossed the big road with the cars and the trucks. Then we went past the houses on the other side where my uncle Pablo lived—you see the houses, the rows? And after the houses we could see the pools. But before the pools—all these rough lines, you see?—was the caña. We didn't like the caña, and we ran very fast, because sometimes we saw the dead bodies lying in the middle of there. The mens come with the knives in the night, and they kill the people living in the houses so no one could hear them. You can see here, the bodies with blood and the throats cut in the caña. Sometimes they were still in the same places when we were finished swimming and ran back, because people were scared to say they knew the dead bodies. It was dangerous to stay very late near the pools, so we always remembered to run home fast before the sun went down in the sky."

María pushed the drawing aside and sat back in her chair. She was silent for a few moments, then continued: "After my mother died, Miguel was supposed to take care of us. He try to find work with his friends; he even went for a little time to the army to get a uniform and bring us food. My mother didn't allow him to have a gun, but after she died he was angry and shot a gun at the sky. Anyway, the uniform was too big for him and he looked funny. Everybody laughed at him, and he never went back. One time he got money from somewhere, and my grandfather teach him how to drink. I was mad because my mother never allowed Miguel to drink, but now he was drunk like the others.

"When we were in the back of the truck and they took us to the orphanage, Miguel say it was only for a little time and he would come back for us. But he lied. He lied because he knew otherwise I would cry and run after him. I saw him one time when they brought the boys from the orphanage to visit us girls. He told me not to be sad. He told me it would only be for a little time and we could be together again. I wasn't sure if I believe him, but now I think he knew it was a lie. He said he try to watch out for Aurelio and I should be together with Ramón. He said there was nobody else anymore to take care of our little brothers.

"One day they took us to an office and told us we would be adopted. Miguel was angry—he wanted all us to stay together. Then they gave him those papers to write on. We never went to school like here, and I think maybe he didn't know how to write his name. That was the last time I saw Miguel."

A Salvadoran boy of twelve or thirteen—Miguel. I often wonder how it was for him when he turned over his younger sister and two brothers to the state orphanages and the Salvadoran courts. I wonder how he felt when he said good-bye to Aurelio and ran away from the boys' orphanage with a friend, knowing that the gringos were coming for the children the next day.

What happened to Miguel? Did he go back to the countryside and join the resistance? Was he picked up on the streets of San Salvador and returned to the orphanage, to be delivered later to the army? Did he illegally slip across the borders to Guatemala, to Mexico, to the United States? Indeed, was he even still alive? I sometimes dream that Miguel flies at night like an angel to our house to confront me with the truth—what is it? Then, stunned by shock and fear, soaked with sweat, I wake up.

The handsome swimming instructor was clearly a familiar, trusted figure to the elite of San Salvador who used the Hotel Presidente as their country club. He led his tiny charges out of the pool to a covered recreation area where they were met by beaming mothers carrying dry changes of clothes. As the children disappeared with their parents into the dressing rooms, chattering happily about newly acquired aquatic skills, the swimming instructor paused for a moment to light a cigarette and have a cool drink before meeting his next assignment—a gymnastics class for preadolescent boys, some of whom were already trotting out of the dressing rooms in their leisure suits.

A loudspeaker attached to the neatly thatched roof of the recreation area began to blare seventies-style disco music, and a score of boys between the ages of seven and ten, at least half of them pudgy, unathletic, and unsure of themselves, swung their arms and kicked their legs in movements somewhere between new-age aerobics and the fitness program of the Royal Canadian Air Force. The instructor, refreshed from his short break, shouted encouraging words while he stood before the young Salvadorans in his swimming trunks, showing off his impressive physique.

It was still early, and except for a few sun worshipers, the gymnastics class, their mothers, and María and me, the poolside area was empty. Then I noticed a group of men in dull brown hotel uniforms sweeping near the cabanas and palm trees on our left. The regular rhythm of the scrape, swish, swish of their brooms came closer, minute by minute, as if threatening to drown out the disco droning of the loud-speaker. A second group of men swept the open grill area surrounded by lush tropical flowers, where the waiters were preparing a buffet.

"Tonight we will have festivities," one of the waiters inter-rupted my dozing as he put our ice-cold ginger ales on the table and wiped a few lingering water spots with a white linen towel. "You must not miss our celebrations," he advised with a polite smile, standing formally with the linen towel folded again over his arm, pointing to colorful streamers and piñatas hanging at regular intervals around the buffet area.

"All this for us?" I joked, scanning the air with my hand to indicate the relative emptiness of the place. It felt comfort-able to hear the clatter of dishes, the informed, regular footstep of a waiter in a white jacket, bending his head just a bit to listen carefully to my broken Spanish, smiling, answer-ing in slow, specialized waiter English. The gratuitous friend-liness of the waiter made me feel relaxed—I was being served, taken care of again. Besides, I had been sitting in ab-solute silence with María for almost an hour. "Yes, Señora," he replied with a warm smile. "But also many people from our city come to El Presidente on the weekend to have good time. We have many good time—good times," he corrected himself.

Two days earlier, at sundown, the Novaks and I had arrived here in a taxi from the airport. As we approached the edge of the city, human figures moved endlessly up and down and across rocky inclines, on meandering paths, around tight clusters of wooden and aluminum shacks piled one next to the other, hardly visible as night began to fall, melting into the red-hot glow of scattered wood fires. Here and there, again and again, in a landscape that knew no escape and no end, women and girls worked around the fires while men and boys brought the last bundles of wood. It was the bitter smell of the city, burning wood and burning food, the global twilight of the urban poor. All around there was not a voice, not a sound, only silence.

Soon we had left the shantytown, and the taxi wound through an elegant middle-class suburb. Orderly, with locked gates, closed shutters, and attractive front gardens, the residential streets smelled of tropical flowers, bleeding. There was not a soul on the sidewalks, only silence. Silence. All at once I saw the glimmer of lights in the distance. Only one more turn, one sharp incline, and we reached the large bright entrance of the Hotel Presidente with the familiar sight of taxis and sleek, shiny cars parked in front. Then we were greeted by doormen, bellboys, decals for Diner's Club, Bank of America, American Express.

Swish, swish, scrape, scrape—the swishing and scraping of the brooms came closer now. One of the men—small, lean, his wrinkled, leathery face concealing the intensity of many such mornings—looked up and offered a hint of a smile. I took it in and smiled back at him. Then I looked across the table at María. Her face had softened—she had just finished Ramona's last outfit and was trying it on the cardboard doll. Toward my right, I looked at the shining, sweaty faces of the boys in the gymnastics class, about to be dismissed. Exhausted and bored, a couple of the boys stared curiously at us.

Then I saw it as never before! Then I understood fully what I had experienced heretofore only from a distance. Brown and white—there were only two colors in El Salvador. Vera, the hotel guests, the Novaks, and I were white. The dark-skinned, brown-eyed, black-haired swimming instructor and the waiter were white. But María and her brothers were brown. There were clear limits set, clear borderlines here. Blond-haired, blue-eyed Vera and I were unmistakably like the swarthy, sun-tanned swimming instructor and many of his charges. María and her brothers, like the men in dull brown uniforms sweeping the hotel with their rectangular brooms, were brown. The boys and the swimming instructor knew this; Vera knew it; and María knew it. Now I, too, knew a passageway into the silence. What kind of world was this, made up of henchmen and victims?

CHAPTER

8

Later that afternoon, María and I followed the waiter's advice and looked around the hotel at the fancy decorations for that evening's banquet. She seemed pleased by all the goings-on, much happier now. The band was beginning to assemble under one of the thatched canopies, and a saxophonist and a drummer were rehearsing a number I recognized but couldn't place. The tune followed us as we walked toward the poolside table where we had sat earlier cutting out paper doll clothes.

It was twilight. Except for a few elegantly dressed guests sipping cocktails on the other side of the pool, the area was deserted. I knew I had seen too many black-and-white movies, too many gray palm trees swaying behind a male figure in tuxedo jacket white looking down at a blonde woman in a long chiffon evening gown and pearls. Humphrey Bogart, Ingrid Bergman. There was the promise of moonglow, and for a moment I thought I heard the strains of Glenn Miller.

All of a sudden, on the other side of the fence behind us, two vans screeched to a halt and spilled out twenty people, like an army plane dropping heavily equipped parachutists to the ground. Large, stocky men and women, they were clad in crisp

38

new light blue uniforms, each uniform displaying a huge red cross on the chest. They dispersed and walked—a better word is "marched"—to every dark corner of the pool area, inspected each patch behind the flowering bushes, then banded together again and headed for the hotel terrace. The women, despite the fact that they were wearing skirts and pumps, walked more liked drill sergeants than any Red Cross workers I had ever seen. The men walked like military men.

Yankee itinerary—I didn't want to think about these thugs. I wanted to look away, to deny what was happening. I was a North American with liberal views. I wanted to give these people in a country to the south of us the benefit of the doubt. Maybe they really were from the Red Cross and just happened to be enormous and sullen, just happened to have spanking clean uniforms in a poor, underdeveloped country. Red Cross blue. We were in a luxury hotel in a tropical country; on the surface everything looked like the images of Caribbean vacations in travel brochures. Who was I now? A naive voyager of the heart and mind? A bleeding-heart liberal with an agenda?

I looked down at María. Her face was a blank, silent and rigid. Any interest in music or colorful decorations seemed to have fled before the desire for safety in our hotel room. I held her hand tight. As she had done for two days now, she asked no questions and just followed me.

On the way to the elevators, I remembered to stop at the reception desk to exchange money and arrange for a wake-up call. As we approached the desk, I caught sight of two of the Red-Cross-blue women again, standing in front of a door labeled "Damas," blocking it. A split second later, a third uniformed female emerged from the restroom and joined the two outside. Then they moved to a nearby service room door and repeated the same thing: two of them stood outside, the third went in. On the other side of the lobby, four of their Red-Cross-blue male colleagues marched toward the elevators, then stopped; one of them pushed a button, probably the one to go up.

"Sounds like the Venezuelans!" Months later, a Salvadoran Christian Democrat government official in exile told me that Venezuelan paramilitary groups regularly trained the Salvadoran death squads and liked to flaunt their muscles in such public displays of uniform. "The Venezuelan squads are extremely thorough," he said with a resigned laugh and shake of his head. "What you probably saw was the Venezuelans."

There was no doubt about it; they were looking for people, with or without the consent of the hotel administration. They marched around the hotel like commandos, but nobody seemed the least bit alarmed. That was what so frightened me—everything continued at its normal pace. Did these thugs visit here regularly? Had the bell captain asked them to stop by and check things out before the big banquet that night? Elegantly garbed guests were streaming into the lobby through the front door. After all, somebody needed to make sure there were no bombs in the bathrooms or upstairs hallways to spoil the fun.

We were in El Presidente, one of the three major hotels in San Salvador catering to North Americans. "It will be the best one for you and the children," we were told at the orientation meeting by the parent organization facilitating the adoptions. "You'll be in El Salvador two weeks before the national elections, and it might be too risky at the Sheraton—that's where the American military advisers stay. The journalists stay at the Camino Real, and there's too much commotion in a place like that. So the Presidente is really the best. It's mostly for businessmen and tourists, and families of course." Not seeing anyone in the lobby fitting even one of those descriptions, I gave María what I meant to be a reassuring hug. We had arrived at the reception desk.

"Sure 'nough ma'am, no problem—6 A.M. it will be on the dot," said the lanky young man behind the desk, with hardly a trace of a Hispanic accent, as he wrote down the time and room number with a practiced flourish. "Anything else? How is everything? Oh, you mean the final bill? Oh sure, no problem ma'am, you can pay us in collones or dollars, whatever you like."

"Jim" was inscribed on the nameplate just above the breast pocket of his desk clerk uniform. "Oh yeah, sure, I've been up north, lots of times. We have friends up there, and some uncles and cousins, too." He spoke such fluent English—had he ever attended school in the States? "Oh sure, I just finished college up there in Illinois. I was a business administration major. I'm into hotel management now—you know, just working here at the desk for a while, getting to know the ropes from the bottom and seeing that everything is going fine."

Jim was busy while he tended to my affairs and chatted with me. He put his signature on a piece of paper for one clerk, unlocked the cash box and handed money to another while quickly answering a question from someone in a back room. Jim liked what he did and seemed to be good at it. He was plainly in charge, and so open and friendly and Midwest-trustworthy that I almost lowered my voice to ask him what those Red-Cross-blue people were doing in his hotel. As though he would have told me.

I was saved from temptation by a broad twang nearby, there was no mistaking it: "Jeezus, man, you did fuckin' great today. Raadhadhaadhadhaa . . . didja see how low we got around that one hill? They were runnin' like rabbits. Shi-it.

You keep this up and we'll get the rest of those buzzards to-morrow. Fuckin' great, buddy, you were fuckin' great. Greeeaaaat."

I turned my head to look just as a large hand fell flat on a short, squat shoulder. A tall, blond man with a crew cut, close enough and young enough for me to see the traces of his pimples, stood next to me with his Salvadoran buddy, waiting to talk to the desk clerk.

"Hi Mike, how are ya," Jim said in his friendly manner, giving him a wink as he handed me my money over the counter. Looking at the faded imprints of ancient Salvadorans on the collones bills, I counted it. "Same movie tonight?"

"Yea, man," grunted Mike the crew cut, slamming his hand once more on his buddy's shoulder. "Gaaaaaad, are those tits, and the blonde one's gotta fuckin' ass."

I looked down quickly at María and stroked her hair. "Okay, Mike, that's swell," said Jim a bit nervously now, glancing my way, winking even more briskly at crew cut. "You want the beers tonight? We'll send them up, too."

"Sure thing, man. Come on, buddy," bellowed crew cut, dangling his arm around the Salvadoran as they swaggered away.

I was too stunned to move. I saw rabbits running to hide under rocks in Salvadoran villages, ducking behind bushes on the sides of volcanos. I saw buzzards flying over a field of corpses, buzzards' beaks cutting through children's parched skin, tearing the flesh, exposing the insides of small arms and legs like chickens' to the air.

This wasn't the only North American in the hotel with a military haircut and civilian clothes—the place was teeming with them. They were in front of the elevators, in the restaurant, the bar, the lobby. These men alone exceeded the officially cited limit of fifty U.S. advisers. Surely some of them worked as mercenaries and in covert operations for the CIA. They had worked in Vietnam, and now they were working in Central America.

Mike and his Salvadoran buddy were nearing the elevators—María and I weren't far behind. What if we took the same elevator and looked into each others' eyes? What if I ran into the Red-Cross-blue killers upstairs? If there were trouble, where would I report them? To "Jim"? To Mike the crew cut and his buddy? Determined to make it to our room without mishap, I tipped my head forward and tightened my grip on María's hand.

9

Before long, María was asleep in the darkened hotel room. I was too nervous to sleep or to read, and I turned on the television with the sound lowered. "Dallas" was on. The next channel carried a Latin American soap. Three other channels covered politics—it was election time, just two weeks to go. Perfectly suited for the television medium, the blues, reds, and whites of the Arena Party headed by Roberto d'Aubuisson flowed brilliantly across the screen. I couldn't tell whether it was documentary footage or a commercial: A-RE-NA, A-RE-NA, the people shouted happily as they marched in broad columns to the catchy music, their faces lifted upward, their arms held high, hands in tight fists. Orderly, though not so orderly as the Germans were, they were reminiscent of young Italian fascists of fifty years ago. Like all fascists, they managed to be optimistic and modern in the midst of despair.

D'Aubuisson, over forty years old, marched briskly with the others at the head of the column. His shirtsleeves were rolled tight and high to show the tensed muscles of his upper arms; the open neck of his shirt displayed his throbbing arteries and heartbeat. Blood and power. He showed that he was just a man—yet more than a man. Moving as fluidly as someone twenty years younger, he leapt to the rostrum, smiled the wide smile of confident youth, and exhibited the firm resolve of thug power. Roberto d'Aubuisson—killer of priests, an archbishop, political leaders, workers, and campesinos. Ex-major d'Aubuisson—rumored to kill with a nod of his head. Candidate d'Aubuisson—pocketing the money donated by the rich and sending his death squads out the back door to do their work. I knew enough to understand that every other accusation hurled out of his mouth was "communist." Defeated, I turned off the television.

During the 1980s I heard testimony after testimony about the civil war in El Salvador. I listened to the radio, watched the television news, read newspapers and books, and interviewed eyewitnesses. The more I learned, the more I knew that facts became concealed, suffocated by the marshaling of more facts. In time, I learned to trust María's stories and her pencil drawings.

"We all children watched in front of the big house for weddings and parties. Down here were the lines and the people. They were standing and angry, crying very much for my father. In the middle of them was the box on the shoulders. You see how the box is coming down the road? I don't know all of them who were carrying him, but one of them for sure was my uncle Pablo. He and my father always were together with my grandfather, but now my grandfather was too old to carry, or maybe too sad—he just was standing and watched. And here—you see it?—behind the box all by herself my mother is walking in the black dress. She has the circles all

around her—they are the big balls, because on her face are
the tears.

"Now here I drawed the line where the box is turning up
to the house and we children are waiting. On one side is Aurelio with Ramón, and here next to me Miguel is crying so
much. I don't know why, but when my father die, Miguel
couldn't stop crying. When my mother die, he didn't cry
much, he just was angry and shot a gun at the sky. Maybe he
already cried all his tears. I don't think I understood when it
was happening. Both times I knew I was supposed to cry, and
I tried to cry. But I just felt so lonely and didn't cry much.

"After they brought him inside the big house, everybody
came to the box to say good-bye to our father. I remember it
was a big party. When it was over, our mother took us little
ones to the box. She held us over the glass window to see our
father's face for the last time. First she took up Aurelio, then
she carried Ramón. 'There is your father, remember him'—
that's what she said to them. Then it was my turn and she
held me over my father. You could see how one side of his
face was very dark and pushed in. One part of his chest was
pushed in and dark, too. That's how he was lying for a long
time naked on his chest for everybody to see, but you couldn't
see it anymore after they covered him with the box. I remember when I was hanging so close I saw a tear on the little window, it must have come from my mother. Then she told me
the same words—'There is your father, remember him.'"

María picked up her pencil to reinforce the lines tracing
the route her father's coffin took down the main road, then
up toward the house. My eyes lingered on the circles behind
the coffin that were her mother's tears. "There is a saying—
only the small children can see the spirits of their parents
when they are dead. But it was my tía Olivia who first saw
him. Maybe it was because when they were little they played

together and she took care of my father. Anyway, when Olivia took me out of the house it was dark, and all of a sudden we both jumped because we saw him in a big cloud of white. The next day he came again, this time to me and Aurelio. We stared at him a long time—he was sitting on a bench and he looked happy. Later he came alone to Aurelio in a tree, just sitting up there and smiling, looking down at his little boy. Aurelio called to us in the house to tell us he was there, but when we ran out nobody found him. It's because only the small children see the spirits when their parents are dead.

"Miguel was older—maybe that's why he cry so much. But on the day of the dead we went with our mother and brought flowers to the place of the graves. We looked for the cross, but there were too many dead people buried there and we couldn't find it. Anyway, it was not very strong. It was made of wood and it maybe was knocked over. I remember that's when Miguel stopped crying. That's when he promised my mother that one day he would put a cross there to stay."

CHAPTER

10

On Monday morning we took a taxi directly to the American embassy. A Salvadoran soldier examined our belongings at the outside gate, then signaled us on. No, we had no guns, grenades, bombs; no cameras or other surveillance equipment. As we entered the compound, the Novaks walked in front with the two boys; Maria walked behind Aurelio, ahead of me. Zigzagging between the thick concrete walls, we came to the second guard, who also let us pass.

As we approached the third Salvadoran soldier at the third checkpoint, Aurelio kicked the ground with his right foot and spat. He did it very quickly, but I was sure I saw him. The guard didn't seem to see him— Aurelio must have noticed that he was looking the other way. María and I were the only people who could have seen him kick the ground and spit. Her face was a blank; Aurelio's was, too.

Now Ralph, Doris, and Ramón walked past the guard. Aurelio and María were less than two feet from him, their heads about six inches from his waist, about eight inches from the trigger on the rifle slung over his shoulder. We all had to squeeze past this guard as we had squeezed past the other guards. Aurelio looked straight at the back of Ramón's head, María straight at the back of Aurelio's head. Fixing my eyes on María in front of me, I remembered news photos of Salvadoran children looking at corpses on the ground while soldiers lined the street, of children carrying large bundles of their belongings, walking single file with their parents on mountain paths to escape an army attack on their village, their father in front, their mother in back—as if it were Ralph, or Doris, or I.

Inside the embassy I saw no Salvadoran soldiers, only U.S. Marines talking on telephones, carrying papers, writing at desks. We were directed upstairs, where the office area for visa applications was staffed by civilians—well-dressed Salvadoran women who were able to speak the language of those applying to get out. "Just a moment, please"—one of the women handed us forms to fill out and directed us to the benches on the other side of the room. "Someone will see you as soon as possible."

I sat beside the children on one side, Doris and Ralph on the other. Ralph and I filled out our respective forms while Doris attended to the children. Several faces on the bench opposite us looked up to stare at the strange collection of gringos and Salvadoran children. That bench was where Salvadorans sat to apply for visas, waiting, hoping, to get out legally. I still wore the smile I had put on my face when I conversed with the woman at the counter. As I returned the looks of the Salvadoran faces from the opposite bench, the heat rushed across my temples—I had caught myself face to face with despair.

Ramón swung his legs back and forth. María and Aurelio's legs didn't touch the floor either, but they sat at attention and looked straight ahead, both of them obviously frightened by the embassy's tight-security military atmosphere.

"Look at María's skin. I think she's breaking out in something," said Doris suddenly. Small red blotches had begun to appear on María's arms and legs. On her face they looked like scattered pimples. "It must be a heat rash," Doris assured me, smiling at María. In another situation, Doris would have asked if María usually broke out like this. But we were in El Salvador, adopting two brothers and a sister. Instead of asking the question no one could answer, she examined the hands and knees of the boys. Nothing there. All three of the children were silent, their foreheads bathed in sweat.

"¿Qué son? ¿Sabes tú?" I asked María. No, she shook her head just a bit. No, she indicated she had not had this before. Her forehead was very hot. Did the bumps hurt? Did they itch? I cramped my fingers, making a scratching gesture, and grimaced with my face. No, María shrugged her shoulders. She had retreated. She looked down and was silent. Silent.

What to do? I took María in my arms and rushed to the counter where another well-dressed, immaculately manicured Salvadoran woman approached us from the other side. Taking a quick look at María, she smiled approvingly at me—another North American adoption.

"Please look at these spots. I just noticed them a few minutes ago," I said to her with an air of calm, trying to hide my agitation. "There are so many of them—whatever could they be? Perhaps I could see a doctor."

"I am sorry, here there is no one you can see," the woman said in a kind, concerned voice. "But two streets farther is a very good doctor who speaks English." She went to the desk behind her and returned with his name and address.

"It can't be so bad. Maybe it's just a rash," I said to the woman as I sat María on the counter and slipped the paper with the address into my purse. "It's probably a rash," I repeated, embarrassed by all the attention we were getting from the other clerks and the people waiting on the benches. "But I don't know if she's been sick. Really"—I felt myself visibly shaking—"I don't know much about her at all."

"Ah, but you should see the doctor," the woman assured me in her comforting matronly tone, her simple gold jewelry and the subtle aroma of her perfume lending an air of refinement to the situation. "One never knows what such a problem might be. It is terrible, so many people are sick," she said with a gentle shake of her head, "and there is much disease." Glancing up at María's face—her frown, her sweaty forehead, her large, frightened eyes—the woman quickly lowered her head and whispered to me: "We have many dead people here. Nobody buries them for days, they lie in the streets. You don't know where the girl has been. Imagine the infection and disease carried by the animals and the people. If you don't know much about the girl, you really must see a doctor."

"Yes, yes, of course I will. That's right, I really don't know anything about her," I whispered back, equally frightened and confused. While the woman excused herself to consult the U.S. official in charge of the case, I consoled myself by smoothing back María's hair and wiping her forehead with a tissue. She appeared inconsolable. I looked into the mystery of her frightened yet seemingly trusting eyes. No, it couldn't be true, it couldn't be a disease, I tried to assure myself. Still, it was best to see a doctor.

A vice consul agreed to see us right away. I was suddenly struck by the thought that María might not be allowed to come to the States if she were seriously ill. Bathed in perspiration, she sat absolutely rigid on my lap in the vice consul's small office. A disease didn't come on like this, I told myself. Surely this was a psychosomatic reaction. María was just terrified, that was all. Oh it was just her fear, I reassured myself, hugging her rigid body.

Tall, handsome, and wearing a bright pink button-down Oxford cloth shirt, the vice consul entered the office and addressed me with "Hi! How are you today?" I returned the greeting, thanked him for seeing us so quickly, and decided to forgo a reference to the red spots on María's skin. Not seeming to be perturbed by much of anything, the vice consul quickly turned to the visa application. Clearly, everything had been perfectly prearranged by the Salvadoran juvenile court system and its contacts with the adoptive parent organization back in the States. Our appearance at the embassy was perfunctory.

"Looks just dandy!" the vice consul said when he was finished, slapping the papers together and leafing quickly through my passport. Then he signed the papers, affixed the necessary stamps, and stood up to congratulate me. We shook hands, and he showed us back to the waiting room. Relieved that María had her visa and that the vice consul hadn't detained us on the suspicion of any insidious disease, I almost forgot the piece of paper in my purse with the doctor's address.

As María and I walked quickly along the corridor and down the stairs, we passed two more uniformed Marines. My mind spun with swirling benches, despairing faces, warm matronly smiles, and the bright pink Oxford cloth shirt. María's rash was very visible now. She kept her eyes fixed about three feet ahead of her, straight at the floor—a learned, practiced gaze, unchanging as we walked down the last corridor.

CHAPTER

11

A small steel bell sounded as we entered the pediatrician's office. A nurse came out to tell us we had to wait for a while—the doctor was busy and there was another patient ahead of us. I smiled at María and squeezed her hand. She still seemed very frightened, but she heaved a deep sigh and her eyes smiled back at me. Everything in this waiting room seemed wonderfully calm, incredibly quiet. After we sat down on two of the straight-backed chairs nearest the nurse's door, María busied herself with Rosita. I had time to sit back, relax, and melt into the room.

I scanned the chairs lin-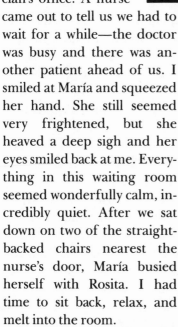ing three of the walls of the small white room, and found the only other patient— an infant held by its nursemaid, the mother sitting beside them. The two women looked occasionally at the baby, smiled at each other, then stared straight ahead. The mother, a tall foxlike creature, her light brown hair falling casually to her shoulders, sat closer to me, only three chairs away. She wore delicately applied makeup and a loose silk designer outfit—proper attire for a lady in any modern city: New York, Paris, Buenos Aires, San Salvador. She crossed and uncrossed her legs repeatedly, and the top

53

leg swung back and forth in jerky rhythm. From the toes of
that top foot hung a flat Capezio shoe, flapping back and
forth against the heel. She held her hands in her lap, turning
each long finger while she examined her salmon-colored
nails—carefully manicured, but recently the objects of nervous biting.

Sitting absolutely straight, her feet planted firmly on the
floor, the Indian nursemaid rocked the baby in a huge white
padded bunting with fine lace trimming, the kind that went
out of fashion in Europe after World War II. When our eyes
met, she sent me the same sweet smile she gave the mother
and the baby. Then her face relaxed for a moment as she
contemplated María. When she caught my eye again—who
knows what she was thinking?—she once again gave me her
sweet smile. Tucking at the lace of the baby's bonnet, adjusting the little strap under the baby's chin, she held the foot end
of the bunting with her left arm, down and away from the
mother, while the head of the bunting was held up toward
the right, so that the mother could peek in to smile at the
baby whenever she wished. The nursemaid was impeccably
dressed in strong white nurse's shoes, a stiff hospital-blue
blouse with puffed sleeves caught at the elbow, and a light
blue and white starched jumper crossed with wide white
straps in back. On her head she wore nothing but a circle of
the fattest, shiniest dark brown braids I had ever seen.

I looked down at María's dull, short, badly trimmed, di-
sheveled hair—despite another washing that morning, despite the careful combing and the pink barrettes. A few
months later, in the States, when her hair had grown a few
inches and I was able to create a variety of ponytail styles for
her, I learned to put the comb aside and part her hair with
my bare hands, as she showed me—this was how it had been
done by her mother. No, I assured María every morning,

there would be no more painful lice and deadly parasites, no more open wounds, no more cutting of her waist-length hair, no knives scraping into the tissue of her scalp by doctors and nurses at the clinic. No, in a few months, her hair would rush down her back once more, like a river.

Now the bangs were pasted with sweat to her forehead, but it didn't seem to bother her. She was tending to pink-cheeked, platinum-haired Rosita, wrapping her in a blanket invented from one of the skirts I had brought for her. Her hands and fingers moved quickly, adjusting a flap around the legs, tucking a stray piece of cloth under the chin. She rocked the doll and hummed quietly. Just a touch higher with her elbow, another few tucks in the cloth here and there, a brush of her index finger on Rosita's cheek—

Oh yes, oh yes! Now I saw it! María was cocking her head, sitting in the same way, looking at Rosita, rocking her, and humming to her in the same way. She was in perfect tune with the nursemaid who was rocking and humming to the baby in her arms. María was a bit rougher and more familiar with Rosita—after all, she was not the lady's, she was her own baby. The nursemaid was kind and gentle, but much more cautious, more rigid with her white charge. María was pulling Rosita up now for a happy swing in the air, giving her an audible kiss, a wide grin, pushing her close to her underarm, snuggling the skirt-blanket around Rosita's body with a playful cuddle of her palms. It was almost as if her rash were disappearing—absurd to have thought it was a disease.

We had been waiting a long time, and the nursemaid's attractive, long-legged mistress had been crossing and uncrossing her legs incessantly. This woman was young, beautiful, rich, surely married to someone with good earning power and family power. She had everything an entire civil war was being fought about, at least on the economic front. Tapping her foot on the floor, drumming her fingers on her knee, she said not a word as she kept up the ritual of peeking at the child and smiling kindly at the nursemaid, the ritual she had learned from her mother, who had learned it from hers. They all had had Indian maids in spanking clean, starched uniforms. Only the length of the skirts had changed.

I put my head in my hands to turn off the image, to tune out the sounds of the tapping, drumming, and swinging of hands, legs, feet. Surely this wasn't merely postpartum depression. This woman knew very well there was a civil war going on right outside her door. She must have been afraid, as one should be afraid in El Salvador. Perhaps she knew too much. Was her husband a lawyer, a landowner, a businessman, a high-ranking military officer—or all of the above? No doubt his wife, this nervous, irritated woman next to me, knew the cost of an elegant dress or a sumptuous dinner in downtown San Salvador. She knew how many hands it took, how many hours, how many heartbeats. It could be that she had learned these things from her maid, or her mother's maid, the people who had silently raised her and now raised her children. She probably knew the price of a European vacation or a weekend in Miami to visit friends and relatives. She knew how many murders it cost, how many lives. Perhaps there was no hope for this woman, unless she went mad.

At last the doctor opened the door, greeted the woman by name, and extended his hand. Visibly relieved, she stood up, gave her hair a practiced, casual shake, and drifted past him through the small white door, followed by her baby in the arms of the nursemaid. Again it was wonderfully quiet. Rosita slept peacefully as María hummed, her legs dangling from the chair, her hands still, no longer fussing with the doll or the skirt-blanket. I rested my head against the wall and dozed, knowing that María's rash was hardly visible any longer, that the spots would soon disappear.

A half hour later, the two women reappeared at the small white door. Once again, the Indian nursemaid held the baby in the padded bunting, as if its body had not at all been extracted from the huge white thing and examined by the doctor. Once again she smiled at everyone, then, carrying the bunting and an enormous navy blue vinyl baby bag, she walked toward the exit. She turned her head back when she reached the door, and waited for her mistress.

Her mistress, meanwhile, was rummaging through her purse, looking for her checkbook. Go on out. Go out ahead of me. Open the door and go on out, she motioned to the nursemaid with a weary hand. The nursemaid turned to the door, put down the baby bag, reached toward the door, and turned the knob. Nothing happened. She turned and turned, but nothing happened. Then she stopped, looked at the baby, rocked it twice, switched the huge padded bunting from her right arm to her left, adjusted the position of her body, and attempted to turn the knob with her right hand. Nothing happened. She tried it again and again, pushing back and forth. The door was jammed. For a moment she stood facing the door. Then she looked over her shoulder at her mistress who had just found her pen and was writing a check.

Out of the corner of her eye, the mother could see that the nursemaid was still there. Go on out. Go out ahead of me. I'll come in a minute, she nodded with her head. Not one word was exchanged. Go on out, she gestured more forcibly now, irritated once again, her face turning into the familiar frown. The nursemaid leaned against the door, pushed at the knob. Then she began rattling, jerking, pulling at the door. A squeak. The baby gave out one squeak, then another. The nursemaid rocked, rocked, and smiled at the little one. The baby was quiet. Obviously relieved, the nursemaid continued to rock with her left arm while directing the right once more toward the knob.

This had been going on for several minutes. Who was I? Where did I stand? The struggle appeared to be going on inside me—what was I to do? I knew only that I wanted to go up to this Indian woman, look deep into her eyes, and weep. I wanted to weep for days, for weeks. I wanted to tell her how beautiful I thought she was, how I had hope when I sat in a room with her. I wanted to tell her I didn't want the bombs, the guns, the helicopters, and that I didn't hoard my money either. We should have just enough to get by. I wanted to tell her that I didn't know what would be, but whatever became of us, María and I would remember her. I realized then that through her I wanted to reach back to María's mother.

Someone else must have pushed me—I wasn't the one. I stood up from my chair and walked to the door, put both my hands to the doorknob and shook it, back and forth, back and forth. Then I drew my body back, got a firm grip on the handle, and pulled as hard as I could. The door opened. Really, there was no drama in it at all. We looked at each other, a bit awkwardly both ways, and smiled. She walked out—I would never see her again. I went back to my chair and sat down.

Engrossed in Rosita, María had apparently not seen a thing, but the baby's mother had witnessed the entire scene. Oh no, you shouldn't have done that, she smiled generously. I am so sorry for your trouble, that was such a nice thing for you to do. She slipped the check to the secretary. Really, I shouldn't have let you do that, but there is so much in my head—so many appointments, so many responsibilities, so much confusion. She gathered up her Pandora's purse, closed it shut, and backed toward the door. Yes, oh, thank you, she nodded. Oh, but I should have taken care of this myself, finished with all these things long ago. Please accept my sincerest thanks, she smiled graciously and gave a last nod. She turned on her heel and her hair swung wide. The door closed behind her.

Now the secretary opened the white door and beckoned us to come in. María stood up cautiously, for Rosita was fast asleep. "Ah, no problem. It is only a rash," said the doctor after he had examined María. "This little girl simply has sensitive skin!" Then he applied an ointment and wrote out a prescription for the same ointment, readily available from the apothecary next door. I remembered to put on more ointment when we returned to the hotel.

At home, back in the States, the pediatrician was of the same opinion. "Sure, it's hard to tell. You say that there are other reasons, and so, sure, it could be an emotional reaction. But let me tell you, lots of children have sensitive skin. Just apply an ointment, any over-the-counter variety. Don't worry," he assured me. "She'll be fine."

So, whenever there was an overload of memories, dreams, or when, for example, a state trooper stopped me for speeding on the freeway and looked into our car to ask for my credentials, María quickly developed a rash. Then I would open my purse, or go to our medicine cabinet, or make a dash for the nearest pharmacy, and apply the recommended ointment to her skin.

CHAPTER

12

Doors slammed and the taxi pulled away from the Presidente. We were off on our way to the airport. Ralph was in front with Ramón on his lap, next to the driver. Doris and I sat in back, Aurelio and María between us. The carry-on bags were at our feet and on our laps, the suitcases in the trunk.

I was glad to be leaving. I wanted to go home. It was 6 A.M., sunrise, and the taxi wound through the familiar tropical treelined streets of the suburban section around the Presidente—it could have been Acapulco or Nice. Then we passed through the outer edges of the city—the people, the poverty. Finally came the rolling landscape, the bushes, the hills. I closed my eyes.

Soon the sun blazed in the eastern sky, obliterating the pain of detail. As the taxi stopped at the first military checkpoint on the highway, one of the soldiers bent down to look through the rear door window. I glanced quickly at María, who was preoccupied with Jennie and Rosita. They were resting together now, under one skirt-blanket, sleeping. We were obviously Americans on our way to the airport, so there would be no further search. The soldier drew a quick circle in the air with his rifle to indicate we could pass.

Between this and the next checkpoint, I allowed myself

to look at the countryside, recognizing it from newspaper and television images, as though I had known it forever. A highway bordered by wooded inclines where guerrillas lie in ambush, I had heard the reporter say in a clipped voice just a week earlier on the evening news. The screen had shown three guerrillas casually dressed in uniforms taken from dead army soldiers. Grinning proudly for the camera, each of the teenagers held a captured M-16 rifle and waited on a dirt road for the next army convoy to pass.

The orange-brown landscape dotted with green patches swept backward past our car. We had time to watch, to listen, to look out the window at our left, past Doris dozing in the corner behind the driver. Aurelio, María, and I—three heads in a row: one small, one just a bit bigger, one very big. The landscape was flooded by the yellow morning light. The air was still. Except for the sound of a passing car, this world of dawn was bounded by silence.

One by one, on the opposite side of the road, figures appeared: two women, a man, a few children. Again a couple of women, a few men, two or three children. Each person carried something with his hands, on her head, and so on, again and again. They walked in single file: barefoot, slowly, firmly, not with stooped shoulders. No one seemed to talk. They walked looking straight ahead, one after the other. The women and girls carried wide jugs on their heads. The men and boys carried wood. Suddenly the landscape was empty. Just as abruptly, the roadside was dotted with colors once again. Ever so slowly, the dots filed silently past our car, which was speeding in the opposite direction.

Ralph reached excitedly for his camera and began to snap pictures. On our way in from the airport it had already been much too dark. Yes, we were in the tropics, in a Third World country. The women's dresses were colorful; the flow of human colors against the warm, dusty landscape appeared exotic. The jugs were deep and wide, the people graceful. But where were they going? How long would they have to walk? There was not a sign of a village, not even a shack. The last two little girls carrying jugs on their heads could not have been older than six. This must have been how María walked with her mother, I told myself, before she came to the orphanage. One of the women photographed from afar by Ralph could have been a sister, an aunt, a grandmother. Oh, the dull fingers and savage bellies of El Norte. If North Americans were childless, did El Salvador have to make up for that, too? I sank back in my seat and looked down, surprised at my sudden sense of shame. Reality was hidden, hidden from our view.

~~~~~~~~~

"*My mother and my tías* carried the big ones, and I had a small pink. It was plastic and light, but not so light on my head when we came back from the spring and it was filled up with water. Oh, we washed our clothes at another place at the river. That was where we liked to splash in the water, and our mother washed us with soap. But we had to watch out. Our mother told us not to go to the very dark place near the water because there was the beautiful woman, the Siguanaba. Watch out, watch out, she lived in a house near the river with her son Cipitio. He made sounds like music and ate ashes at night. His eating was loud, very loud. It woke us up in the night in our houses, we could hear him. But watch out, watch out for the Siguanaba. If somebody stayed too long at the river, and if he was looking too much and feeling her beauty and wanting to keep it, or he came very near and reached for her to touch her—then she turned around just like that and frightened him to death with her horrible face! It was long dirty hair and an old ugly face under her hood. And inside her long silky white dress was her ugly terrible body. Watch out, watch out for the Siguanaba. Somebody tried to touch her one day. They found him dead in her very dark place at the river—she made him die of a fever. The Siguanaba lived close by in the forest with her son Cipitio, and he made sounds like music and ate ashes at night. Watch out, watch out for the beautiful Siguanaba. Watch out!"

Aurelio and María were scanning, searching the countryside. Every few minutes Aurelio turned to look at his sister, but neither of them said a word. Aurelio didn't have two dolls on his lap under a skirt-blanket. He didn't know how to play with dolls, and each of his hands was placed carefully on a thigh, palm up, holding nothing. The warm light of the morning sun forced him to half close his eyes, keeping him from seeing the void. María looked out the window with Aurelio, her eyes naked, waiting for him to cry. Now both of them were squinting and searching, for they must have known that this was the last ride. Slowly the morning sun buried the shadows of the past. The children's eyelids shriveled at the brightness of the countryside.

On the route connect- ing San Salvador with the fine surfing beaches of the Pacific, the ambitious new international airport lay fairly idle in goat-grazing country. Its airstrip could not be compared to that of the notorious Ilopango military base, which housed U.S.-donated aircraft, but it was impressive. Grafted onto a preindustrial countryside and expressing an imperialist vision of the future, the civilian airport had the potential to support even bombers and combat transport planes.

The taxi unloaded us in front of the main entrance, and we carried our bags and suitcases to the Taca Airlines counter. Armed soldiers posted at regular intervals seemed to outnumber the civilians working here. As we waited in line at the counter the children deliberately stayed close, as if stuck to us. I remembered the four North American churchwomen who had been killed by army soldiers near the airport three years earlier. They must have walked through these very main doors on the late afternoon of their deaths. Two of the nuns had arrived on a plane; the other two women had driven in a van to meet them. The same van was found the next day near their mutilated bodies, one piled on another with just enough dirt on top to cover them fully—a grave in the style of the right-wing death squads.

As we walked toward the gate area, I recalled the newspaper photograph of the U.S. ambassador at the site. Dressed in a white oxford cloth shirt and cotton trousers, his hands on his hips, he looked down into the grave while the bodies of the women were hauled up by ropes. That picture appeared on the front pages of newspapers around the world the next day. The U.S. ambassador and the corpses—now we believe what we see. After he complained to the military, Ambassador Robert E. White was harassed by right-wing demonstrators outside his house in suburban San Salvador. Soon he was recalled by Ronald Reagan, who had just been sworn in as President. His experience in El Salvador must have changed Ambassador White's life. How would this voyage change mine?

Despite the confusion of people, the procedures at the gate for Miami were quick and efficient. Most of the people milling around the gate were North Americans—tall, lean, sunburned white men with crew cuts. Interspersed among them were shorter, darker, muscular young men clad in crisp short-sleeved shirts and khaki pants and wearing elaborate digital wristwatches. These were not all together, but in ones and twos, some of them apparently traveling with the North Americans. Newspaper pictures of American military advisers and Salvadoran special forces trained in Georgia and North Carolina flashed across my mind. Why should they be traveling on Taca Airlines, not on a military transport? Should I doubt my perceptions? I wasn't sure.

Again I felt the fear that would accompany me from now on. Not the familiar flutter of anxiety about getting to know the stranger who had become my daughter, but the deep, dull fear of having entered the consciousness of the war zone, with no exit in sight. Confronting the killer on a personal level—face to face on the street, in a hotel, on a plane, in the next seat.

Sitting across from us at the gate, a pretty young woman of about eighteen in a pastel blue shirtwaist dress sat demurely next to a young man with a crew cut who was dressed in a sports shirt, trousers, and jogging shoes. His arm reached casually around her shoulders, and he seemed to be whispering sweet nothings in her ear. She blushed, while her fingers fondled the small diamond on the ring finger of her left hand. They were obviously North Americans—young Joe Doe and his sweetheart from Hometown, U.S.A. He was empty-handed; the pink luggage left little room for speculation as to whose it was. Apparently she was traveling back to the States and he was more or less permanently stationed in El Salvador, possibly teaching Salvadoran pilots to maneuver Huey helicopters or the A-37s that dropped bombs on Salvadoran peasants each day. How much of this was known, would ever be known, to the pretty young woman in pastel blue from Hometown, U.S.A.?

María was dressed for the trip in a white blouse and pink jumper. The last photograph from our journey showed a close-up of her. The gray shoulder strap of her unicorn purse was visible, and she looked toward the left-hand side of the photograph, showing a three-quarter face, relaxed shoulder, serene eyes, a faint smile. I came to think of it as my snapshot version of the Mona Lisa, except that there were no jagged rocks, no dark green, brown, black sky in the background. There was only the clear glass of the large gate window at the El Salvador airport, displaying baggage carts and the red, white, and blue tail of the Taca Airlines plane waiting for us outside.

Inside the plane we sat in two rows. Doris was next to the aisle, Ramón in the middle, Ralph at the window. Behind them sat María at the window, Aurelio in the middle, I on the aisle seat. As the plane waited on the runway, María and Aurelio began to color feverishly in the coloring books the stewardess had given them. In the middle seat in front of them, Ramón laughed and squealed, delighting his new parents.

As the plane left the ground, I stared at the back of Doris's seat—I didn't know how to make this separation. Aurelio's and María's heads were hidden in their coloring books, and splashes of green, yellow, and red appeared on the pages. Soon I heard the ping when the no-smoking sign went off, then a bit later the seat-belt sign was turned off, too. My mind registered the aroma of cigarette smoke from the rear and the familiar sounds of an airplane cruising at high altitude. I could hear the buzz, smell the cigarettes, feel the pressure on my sinuses from the dry air. My eyes were heavy, and I dozed on and off.

High up in the air, with a spectacular view of the Guatemalan mountains, I let my eyes drift toward a man with a rust-colored crew cut sitting farther ahead across the aisle with his wife and three teen-

age children. In the States he could have been the model as-
tronaut with his model family, model green lawn, and tract
home. Here, as we were propelled northward, leaving El Salvador permanently, or semipermanently, behind, his bright
yellow polo shirt and plaid cotton slacks made me think of
death.

After staring at the back of his clean-shaven, sunburned
neck for too many minutes, wondering what exactly he did in
El Salvador to make him secure enough to have brought his
entire family with him, I went to the back of the plane to light
up. Ralph followed me. We smiled at each other, smoked, and
exchanged stories about how we had been trying to kick the
habit. Doris was in her seat with her head back and her eyes
closed. On the way down, she had vomited before each land-
ing, and this trip rekindled her agony. By the time Ralph and
I returned to our seats, the descent to Belize was well under
way. I held a damp paper towel to Doris's brow, and Ralph put
the paper bag close to her mouth. All she could do was gag.

Belize appeared to be jungle, nothing but jungle. A few
rusted jeeps, trucks, and small planes were parked at odd an-
gles along the tiny airstrip. They were a faint yellow-green,
reminders of the reluctant demise of another colonial power,
the British, who left here in 1945. Soon after the plane
stopped in front of the airport building—there were no
docking gates here—I heard commotion and laughter at the
door. Missionaries working in Belize, I overheard the stewardess say to the man across the aisle from me. They bustled
cheerfully past me down the aisle with their full beards,
broad-brimmed hats, flowing skirts, and open faces, waving
gaily at the people outside the airport entrance who were waving back even more generously and wishing them a good trip.
None of the missionaries had the stern, apprehensive look of
those of us who had entered this plane in El Salvador. It was

as if we had come from another world, from an entirely different sensibility and era.

The children had been coloring feverishly in their coloring books ever since the plane had sat on the runway at the San Salvador airport, but only now did I acknowledge to myself that they had also been talking to each other in low voices. As the plane sped down the runway, I heard Aurelio speaking quickly and quietly to María. Gesturing, arguing, explaining, he appeared to be relating a series of events. His arms and hands and head moved to reinforce his point. María listened intently, now and then asking a question or interrupting to comment. Both of them spoke in clear, precise, adult tones, not at all in the shy, cute baby voices they had been using with the Novaks and me in their one-word answers. They continued to talk hastily, as if this three-hour flight between El Salvador and Miami were their only chance for language between the past and the future. Soon memory and words would fade for them both.

I managed to pick up a word or a phrase here and there, but couldn't put it in context. Aurelio was very excited now. It was something important, something big. María was listening intently, taking it all in. Then she started. She was off on her own story, and he was listening, caressing, grabbing at her every word. Her words carried the same sober tone, the same speed, the same sense of seriousness and urgency.

This was my daughter. This was the language, the story of my daughter. She had lived thousands of words, thousands of years. Words, memories, stories, explosions, pictures. How long would she remember? How much would she be willing to recount? I heard the name Miguel. Just as often I heard the word *marta*. What did that mean—marta? I heard nouns and verbs I recognized, but couldn't put them together. Really, I didn't understand a thing. This was the first time I

had heard the children really speak, and for the first time I
understood how many words separated them from us—how
many showers of words, unspoken words, never-to-be-spoken
words.

For a split second, María's eyes caught mine. Without a
hint of recognition, she turned her head away and bent forward toward her coloring book. Her right hand began the
jerky motions again; Aurelio did the same. They were silent.
I stared blankly at the print in my book—it was someone's au-
tobiography. After a while the stewardess stood over me with
three trays of food. Aurelio and María paused. Signaling that
they didn't need any help from me, they began to talk quietly
while they ate. I straightened up and put the napkin in my
lap, determined to concentrate on my food.

When I was finished, I read through the Salvadoran business weekly in English that had been offered to me by a
distinguished-looking man sitting across the aisle. Gray-
haired and portly, he was apparently married to the Latina
woman about fifteen years younger sitting next to him. They
conversed in hushed voices in English. A gracious, refined,
impeccably dressed couple, obviously caring for each other—
it was soothing to be near them. They must have been aware
of the brutal killings in El Salvador, I told myself. They must
have thought at least once in a while about the fate of the victims. In the business paper, I read columns on crops, invest-
ments, and U.S. technology. There were charts of prices and
statistics, but no mention of the dead. Were the children orphans from the streets of San Salvador, or from the
countryside? Good God, I thought to myself, I didn't even
know that much! I put down the paper, yielding to the wave
of exhaustion that came over me.

I rested my head against the seat and tried to keep my

eyes closed, but it was a strain, and they opened every thirty seconds or so against my will. I could feel Aurelio checking now and then to see if I was listening. Satisfied, he continued. That was right, I wasn't listening. I didn't understand a thing, except that I didn't understand. There I was, situated midway between the children's agitated Spanish whispers and the subdued conversation coming from across the aisle. Drained and feeling quite forlorn, I turned my body toward the aisle and prayed for sleep.

There was irregular tension in the seat belt—I was awakened by a jolt. We had hit some air pockets, and there was commotion in front of me. Ralph reached something across Ramón in the middle seat, toward Doris. She was vomiting again, this time even before the descent. "It's okay," Ralph squeezed his head between the two seats to reassure me. "This time she doesn't feel so bad. She doesn't need anything—it's not so bad this time."

The children were quiet. María was still coloring, while Aurelio sat back in his seat, looking sick and glaring at the ceiling. "¿Te sientes mal?" I asked him, pointing to my stomach. He nodded. "¿Al lavabo?" Yes, yes.

We rushed to the lavatory. I opened the door, raised the lid of the toilet, pointed to the bowl, and within seconds Aurelio expelled his entire breakfast and whatever else he had had that morning. We found the paper towels and wiped and cleaned up together. Aurelio was feeling bad, and, even worse, embarrassed, but then the plane, bumping along the air pockets, sent our bodies rushing, crashing into lavatory obstacles, Aurelio's on the level of sink and toilet, mine against the upper walls. We giggled and laughed so loud that we both tried to cover our mouths with our hands, but the rushing and crashing made it impossible. Then, we collapsed on the floor. Oh, what a riot! It was unbelievably funny, and the tears rolled down our cheeks.

We managed finally to get up and open the door, swaying and bumping our way along the return to our seats. Doris had stopped vomiting. Her head was tilted back against the seat, her eyes barely open. Aurelio gave her, then María, a wide, toothless grin.

We had said our awk- ward, reluctant good- byes, promising we would see each other as often as possible in the months and years to come. Then the Novaks and the boys disappeared into a plane that took them from Miami airport to a home port 300 miles from our destination. "Now we're on the last leg of our journey," I said to María as we turned away, and she smiled at me even though she didn't understand the words. We had a two-hour wait for our plane, and we spent the time crisscrossing the termi- nal, browsing in gift shops, eating hamburgers and fries, and sprawling in the big, com- fortable chairs in the lounges.

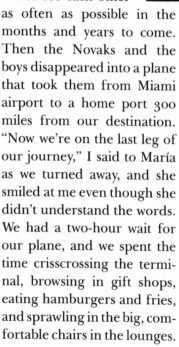

A young Latina woman stopped to talk to María. "Oh, such a pretty one," she said, tipping her finger under María's chin. "Such a sweet one," she smiled at me, turning her eyes again toward María. Then the woman be- gan to chitter-chatter in Span- ish, saying sweet, lovely things that María liked to hear but had probably not heard in a long time. Her face was flushed, and she savored every look, every word. She lowered her eyes, answered in almost inaudible monosyl- lables, and was happy.

"¿Qué es 'marta'?" I asked María. We were sitting at the gate now, ready to board, playing the word game in which each of us asked what something was in the other's language. I had told María that azúl meant blue, amarillo was yellow, rojo was red, and that cabeza, pelo, and ojos were, respectively, head, hair, and eyes. She, in turn, had given me the Spanish names for articles of clothing and hair accessories. Now, remembering the word she and Aurelio had so often used when they talked on the plane, I asked her what "marta" meant. We were both worn out, but relaxed and happy.

María started to giggle. "¡Qué es Marta! ¡Qué es Marta!" she repeated, mocking my accent, laughing, slapping her thigh. "¡Qué es Marta!" Obviously, to her it was hilariously funny. "¡No qué! ¡No qué! ¡Quién! ¡Quién! ¡Quién!" she shouted.

"Okay," I conceded. "Quién, then." Who, not what. "Okay—Quién. ¿Quién es Marta? ¿Quién es?" I asked playfully, wondering to myself at the logic of the grammatical construction.

"¡Marta!" shrieked María, succumbing for the next several minutes to further giggles and laughter. "Marta es mi hermana," she said finally. "Mi-her-ma-na," she pronounced loudly and clearly, pausing at the end of each syllable in case I still didn't understand.

"What! Oh, oh my God! Oh, I didn't know you had a sister. I didn't know."

Oh yes, oh yes, María told me in a steady, enthusiastic stream of Spanish words, of which I understood only a fraction. Marta was her sister, much taller, much older. Marta was very pretty, a little fat. Once she had very, very long beautiful hair to her waist, but after she left home she cut it shorter. Sometimes she wore pants, but for parties she wore a special yellow dress—it was so pretty! Marta had a baby. She had many babies, and her belly had been large three times. Marta had a husband, but no longer. He was dead. María made the

sign of the slashed throat with her index finger. Two of the
babies were dead, too. "Muertos. Dos. Dos muertos." But
Marta's little girl was cute and pretty. "¡Muy, muy bonita!"
Her name was Marinita. María beamed at me, remembering
how cute and little Marinita was.

"¿Dónde está Marta? ¿Dónde está?" I was finally able to
interrupt.

"Yo no sé. No sé," María replied, looking entirely calm
now, her face suddenly blank. No, she didn't know where her
elder sister was, had no idea where she could be. She
shrugged her shoulders and looked down at her feet, crawling into the awful silence once again. No, no, she didn't know
anything. She couldn't remember. Marta?—no, she didn't
know any more.

<hr />

At the end, María told me much later in the States, her sister
Marta lived with her husband's family in a hamlet called El
Chile and worked in the coffee fields. María said that Marta
cried out and swooned when she entered the shack on the
edge of the city and saw her dead mother. She had to be re-
vived three times with a flask before she was able to walk to
her. Then María watched Marta put on the black dress her
mother had worn only a few months earlier to mourn their
father. Since then Marta, too, had become a widow and lost
the second of her three children. Now she was the eldest, and
her mother's bequest to her was the black dress.

According to María, her mother's eyes didn't close for
three days—she didn't want to leave her children in their
grief. But on the third day she allowed her three youngest,
one after the other, to close them. "My mother must have

thought it was time, her spirit was ready." María watched her sister Marta cry, but didn't cry for her mother herself. "I knew I was supposed to cry, and I tried to cry. But I only felt my heart break and I was quiet."

After they buried their mother nearby—María didn't know where it was, it doesn't matter—Marta went back up the volcano to El Chile. It was the middle of the coffee harvest, and María and Miguel would have to watch out for their two younger brothers. It was too dangerous to take children up there, Marta said to María.

That was in November 1982. María has never seen Marta again. Three years later, according to a Central America specialist, National Guard troops razed the hamlet of El Chile where Marta lived. The command, according to one of the men who left the Guard soon thereafter, had been to "kill everybody and burn everything in sight—chickens, dogs, babies, anything that's alive." Several of the Guardsmen were said to have gone mad afterward, if not before. Marta may have escaped in time to a zone held by the guerrillas or been confined to a refugee camp during one of the army sweeps forcibly evacuating the area. They say it's almost impossible to locate people like her. María doesn't have much hope that she is alive, and we rarely talk about Marta anymore.

~~~~~~~~~~~~~~~~

It was 7:30 P.M. when we boarded the plane. I had traveled the precipitous route from the north to the center; now I was bringing María from her world back to mine. But dreams move more slowly than the restlessness of time. By the time the plane took off from the runway, María was already dozing, comfortably settled with Rosita and Jennie in the window seat. Then I noticed that we were not alone. An elderly white woman dressed in a seersucker traveling suit sat next to me reading a paperback mystery. Once we were up in the air she put her book in her lap, looked across at María, asked me a few questions, and waited for me to talk. For the first time in five days, I talked about myself. I told the stranger where I was from, where I had been, and whom I had brought with me. I told her how it was, for I knew she would keep my secret.

For the next two hours we talked while María slept, her head resting against a pillow on the black night window, Rosita and Jennie nestled in her lap. She never saw the stranger, as the woman had said goodbye and moved far ahead to the front by the time the plane landed at our destination and María woke up. But on our front step the next morning stood a huge box filled with colorful blouses, skirts, dresses, a pair of ballet slippers, and roller skates. "Who did this for me?" María's eyes seemed to say as she pulled the charmed items one by one out of the box and gazed at them in pure delight. "They're from your fairy godmother," I said to her in broken Spanish. "Madrina," I said with a wink. "Madrina mágica."

During the first year of her life in her North American house, María awoke carefully from her dreams every morning. Then she got up, washed, dressed, and made her bed. Each day she laid her dolls on the bedspread, face up, staring at the ceiling. First Rosita and Jennie, and Hug Me who was waiting for her that first morning. Then three smaller dolls directly below them. In two rows they rested, face up, directly above, below, and next to each other. Three heads in a row; three heads in a row.

Face down, on top of each doll, María placed one of her stuffed animals. She had just enough—six. One unicorn, one lamb, two bears, one rabbit, one panda. The larger animals lay on the larger dolls in the top row; in the bottom row lay the smaller animals on the smaller dolls. Each day, all day, they lay in that position, one on top, one on the bottom—holding, loving, protecting each other. Six heads in a row; six heads in a row.

At night, the dolls and the stuffed animals sat together at the foot of the bed and waited for morning. Except for Rosita and one stuffed animal, and one other doll—they all got a turn—who were allowed to sleep in the bed with María. Four heads in a row.

"*Oh, I heard them.* My parents were only a pinch away from me on the bed and I heard them. They tried not to make even a sound, and I pretended I was not knowing at all. I was quiet and seeming to be very asleep, but I knew it. I always knew where I came from, and I knew just how it was when I came out of the big warm belly. My mother told me how it didn't take long. I was almost out and ready, and I started to push. My mother pushed, too, and push, push, both of us pushed. First it was my head and it looked down. I pushed hard with my head, my mother pushed, too. And once more, push, push, and my mother still one more push. Ah, there was my head. Then came my shoulders. All at once slip, slip, and a little more slip—there, my whole body came out. Then my father cried, a girl, oh, oh, it's a girl! He was so happy to have a girl, because after Marta and before Miguel they first had a girl, then a boy. But they lost them, Rosa and Victór; they died of a fever. I know, because my mother told me about Rosa. First everybody cried very much, and then my father made a box. They put Rosa in the box with her dresses— because of the spirit, just in case. Then they put poor little Rosa in the ground, and on the top they put flowers. Anyway my mother told me, now it was a girl's turn again, a good time for a girl. First my father held me up there and cut the tie from my mother. Then he looked all around me and washed me, all slippery and wet, because I worked so hard pushing, especially with my head. Then everybody came to see me, and my father cooked the chicken so my mother's milk would be healthy and strong. I was round and brown and pink, and I had bushy black hair. I made a fist with my hands, and I had the long fingernails. Oh everybody was so happy, because they liked me so much and now I was there.

"When I was crawling and walking a little, I like to hide under my mother's skirt and hold on to her leg. I remember up there was such a big ball in my mother's green dress. The green dress was my favorite. I don't know why, but I liked the green and the white collar and the little round buttons so much. Later they buried the dress with my mother—you know, if the spirit came back, just in case. But when I looked up something was pushing and stretching. When my mother put me close to her belly, I felt the loud thump inside the green dress. I knew the thump from before, from the nights of my father and mother. I knew it from my heart, too. But this was a different heart, this thump was an other. And you know, that was Aurelio.

"My legs were still tiny and trembling when they took me down the three little steps to my grandparents' house. My grandmother Tonia was sweeping and maybe a little bit angry, or just talking to herself. She was loud and wild sometimes, and when she was angry she liked to hit us children with her broom and throw stones at us. Anyway, this time I remember she was just sweeping. I sat on the ground and watched her and waited to go back to my mother. But when it was time I didn't want to see the baby at all. I was afraid he was round and brown and pink, maybe sweet, too. They brought me to the bench and said, look, look, but I didn't want to see him. I know I was angry because I didn't want him even to be there at all. They were all saying, look, look, but I kept my face down and tried not to look. I think I was a little jealous when Aurelio came. I pretended he wasn't there for a long time, and I tried not to look.

"The next time it didn't take long. My mother already did it six times, and she knew how to do it. It was early in the morning. I remember, because my father was outside cooking the water for the chicken and drinking the coffee. I was inside standing next to the bed, watching my sister. Right next to me was the black plastic hanging over the bed to make it private. My mother was in there a long time, it was quiet. All of a sudden we heard the cry from the baby. My father went quick to my mother and cut the tie and washed the baby. After that we all went to my mother and looked at Ramón. Right up close he was sweet and all kinds of colors—pink, too. He was very tiny, but not scary at all. First I thought I was afraid, but I wasn't a bit jealous. Maybe now Aurelio was a little bit jealous, because he didn't want to look. Anyway, there was much hair on Ramón's head, but under the hairs on the top just a slip of skin covered up something. It was open and round, a big hole on top of his head, you could feel it. Ramón was the littlest one of us all. You had to be careful—he was so soft and sweet.

"I was sleeping with Aurelio in the hammock for little ones hanging over our parents' bed. I remember down there on the bed our mother was giving her milk to the baby. But Aurelio was angry and crying, he still wanted her milk. So our mother gave the hammock a push with her leg till Aurelio stopped his crying. I wasn't like that, my mother told me. When the time came I didn't want more, it was enough. I knew I was finished, and I turned my head—no!—from the breast. But Aurelio was still wanting and jealous, or that's what he imagined. But soon he was just hanging and dreaming in sleep in our hammock, and down there the baby was sighing and smiling. Then I liked to climb down to be with my mother, and she told me the stories and I listened to her. That's when she told me about when I was born, and about Rosa and Victór. Oh my mother's sweet voice, I always believed her. Well, not always before with Aurelio. But now it was over. Now my mother liked me to help with Ramón, and to sweep, and to come all the places with her. And now she told me the stories. Oh my mother, I liked again so much to go with her and be close to her."

PART

2

HOMAGE TO CANDIDA

*Cándida, it was the first spring of María's new life
in North America. Each night, with spidery brown fingers, she opened the medicine cabinet in our bathroom
and emptied the Band-aid box, nimbly affixed flesh-
colored (whose flesh color?) tape with white gauze to
her scarred knees, to dolls' joints, to long spiny cracks
running across the eggshell-white walls of our house.
Then, stepping carefully around fractures and wounds,
she took me quietly by the hand, whispering, pointing
here and there, ever cautious, to display the evidence, to
acknowledge the symptoms of healing.*

*Cándida, you must have been a healer. You must
have known the bark, the grasses, the leaves, and the
roots. It was Chinchontepec, your ancestral volcano. It
was your own flesh—the air, the sky, and the back of
that mountain. Your mother still wore the long skirts of
your ancestors and covered her gray braids with a
shawl. This alone was an act of subversion in El Salvador. Yes, as a subversive—wasn't that how she lived
until the end? She would never leave, she was too old to
run. She told you this when you came up there with
your husband and children to warn her of the army's
campaign to raze the area. She could not run and keep
living, she would rather be dead, she said as she stood
before her hut and tiny plot of land with her three youngest children who still lived with her. She had been born
there and lived there, belonged to the earth and the sky
and the mountain, she told you as she plucked one of
her small red tomatoes for María de Jesús. Her grand-
daughter heard her speak quietly to her fields and knew
that she preferred their company to that of most people.
Subversive—isn't that how she was identified the next*

day when she and her twelve-year-old daughter were
among the women and girls raped by government sol-
diers, then put up against a wall with her twin sons and
other villagers next to the local tienda *and killed?*

Cándida, it must have been '49 or '50 when you
and Felipe were running wild in separate yards, kick-
ing at stones, spotting an iguana, or catching a frog or
a lizard. You knew each other or didn't, it didn't matter.
You knew, or would know, that you would love each oth-
er, if not somebody else; that his father was José, hus-
band of Tonia, that your family lived farther up there
in the red clay. They greeted as their parents had
greeted, and theirs. They walked past the same tam-
arindo trees and in the same dust, sweating from the
same heat, working at the same finca *and at some of the*
others, depending on the season, the planting, and
where there was work. So in the midst of all that you
were three or four or five years in all, knowing or not
knowing, it didn't much matter, that you and Felipe
would kick up dust like that and run wild and fast for a
few more odd years. Later, during the hot noon hour of
the day, the sun melted your eyes into a meadow. Then
you must have lain with Felipe in the sweet grasses that
took root on the dusty brown hillside of the volcano.
Alone with him you must have been pleased, surely in
the beginning, even toward the end. By this time you
had spent nearly a lifetime together. Life there for many
was short, and hard, but surely never enough.

Granted, Felipe drank, and the other men, power-
less against the sugarcane fields (machetes, wages, fer-
mented juices), a colonial system plotted by white
landowners in white cotton suits and white hats to yield
the white poison: sweetener for their and their ladies'
coffee. But boots and guns can kill a man quicker than

the sugarcane fields, and one morning they brought
Felipe's tortured body to you. Silence on Chinchontepec,
agony on the volcano. Near your husband's grave you
slept on tears. It was no defense tactic, but an endless
condition—not endless for you. Eight months later
your orange dress absorbed more blood, this time your
own, to silence your tears and still your pain forever.
Listen to villages hammering, hammering.

    Cándida, you bore seven children. Marta, your
eldest and three times a mother, a widow at nineteen,
soon after you, was last seen on the burnt slopes of
Chinchontepec. Victór and Rosa, your second and
third, died from the children's disease of the poor, de-
hydration and fever. "It is cold, very cold when the children die. It is cold and straight," says María. And
Miguel, your gray-eyed son of thirteen, must live on
bones, on bread, running wild somewhere between your
capital city and Los Angeles. But your three youngest—
two boys, one girl—reside in the north among white
strangers. When they are grown, will you know them?
Tall flowers, straight backs, blossoming on the graves—
El Salvador's children.

Hah! Do you remember how at first I struggled
against you? "Cándida, I don't know myself any
more," I complained, "I am obsessed with a dead person." This alone didn't bother me, for I often imagined
I slept in the grave with you. But you and your people
had invaded my house, and you rose from the dead even
when I awoke from my dreams. If I tried to ignore you,
I saw you in María's face, in the movements of her arms

*and legs. I imagined how you walked when I watched
her cross the room, familiarized myself with the rhythm,
knew how you moved your arms and shoulders when she
scrubbed a burnt pan. I understood how you might
have flashed a smile or broken into a frown when she
glared at me out of the corner of her eye. I lived with
you. I knew your flesh and your bones. Whenever I held
María in my arms, I stared into the iris that held your
reflection.*

*I told you at the outset that I wouldn't believe in
ghosts, but early each morning I climbed the stairs to
scribble my lines and talk with you. At midday you
rested, and I went about my duties. Toward evening, after María and I had settled for the day, you rarely
failed to reappear, and so it was most often the three of
us at dinner. Still, you never seemed quite satisfied, always waiting anxiously, expecting something. In time I
understood that you demanded nothing less than
conversion—not only from me. You were extraor-
dinarily resilient, accepting your fate, yet never con-
doning the gravity of the offense against you. This was
no small order, for in the "you," you naturally included
your ancestors, your contemporaries, and your children. And I? Finally, I can say only that I resigned myself to you. To this day, I cannot understand why I felt
no humiliation, only relief. You became, simply and
clearly, a third presence—the language of unearthed
memory that spoke through the voice of my child. Your
child. Our child.*

*You knew that at first I wouldn't understand
María. I was enveloped by her sadness, by your eternal
silence in her. But I didn't yet know anything about
you. How could I have known? European enterprise,
Yankee individualism—I had learned only how to take*

*care of myself. But you had died, a few years younger
than I. This time I understood that death never comes
easily, no matter how much one has seen, no matter
what part of the world one is in. I knew it too well to say
it was another country, or another way of life. I knew it
too well to shut my eyes and say it wasn't mine. Suddenly, it was not so easy to explain conditions with a
theory or a phrase, or to argue about poverty and violence with a flip of the hand. It was no longer conve-
nient to shrug my shoulders and shake my head in
dismay, as though it were a newsbreak between programs. Now I knew it was you who had died, and this
knowledge devastated me. You died early, and violently,
and my heart was afflicted, even though I was happy
that you had left your child to me. It was I, or no one.
Who else could see the hand that stroked her head still?
Who knew the fingers of generations that folded with
hers into mine? Who else would mourn you, or hear
your whispers when your daughter spoke to me?*

*On this globe I belong to a privileged minority,
and I want to come to terms with that. Our trouble is
that we believe we have no place to go, yet search everywhere for new holdings and solutions. We suffer and
conceal ourselves, insisting that we are right, torment-
ing ourselves and each other. We should own up to the
fact that we are small and it is enough, I tell myself,
that our special liking for the power and the whiteness
is finished. Really, I don't know what we are saving for,
or how much we are supposed to accumulate before we
die. Do we plan to wear gray suits and scan computer
screens for a lifetime? Will any of us seriously consider
shooting people to the stars?*

*I am a European-American, a white woman. I
know that we live deep within, right under the heart of*

an armed giant. His armor doesn't allow him to weep, or to grieve, or to feel compassion, even for himself. We carry his heart on the shoulders of our loneliness and our fears, and we feel the depth of his weight in the violence we turn inward. Somebody has to do the work, otherwise we will shrivel up and die. It is true, I want to separate from the whiteness and the power.

Cándida, I used to think I understood, but I cannot hear in María's language, nor do I speak freely in my own. All around me I am wished a good day and assured that everything is fine, while in the privacy of my house the suffering of an entire people is played out each day and each night. There must be a lifeline to connect these things, but I don't know truth in any language. Only the clamor of the stories and the blur of the images invade my mind. I am a shell. Each night the shell fills up with death, each day it surrenders its whiteness and its power. I am the shell where death can stay for a while and rest.

CHAPTER 17

Dishes clattered, the rolls were hot, and the soup was ready. It was early May, 6 P.M., time for dinner. María ran to fetch violets from the backyard and quickly put them in a small vase on the table. Then we sat down, held hands for a moment, and began to eat.

Dinner usually took an hour and a half. María took the spoon, dipped it carefully into the soup, and guided it to her mouth. The silent ritual was performed repeatedly with awe and precision. I looked at her now and then through the steam that rose from the soup in the plate before me. She answered every look with her large brown eyes. We listened to each other slurping the soup, heard the sound of each swallow. Now and then the earnestness of eating turned into a smile.

A large salad came after the plate was scraped to the glaze and the last glittering drops were savored. The obligatory avocado with lemon sat on a separate plate. María carefully halved the avocado, removed the pit, and separated the meat from the shell. She cut five times with the knife, lengthwise. She turned the plate and slowly cut another five times. She squeezed half a lemon around and around, to the last drop; no juice ever got on her fingers. Then she took the fork, picked up a bit of avocado, tasted it, savored it slowly, and smiled. María remembered something; she was happy. She repeated the movement with the fork, carefully, slowly, again and again. Gradually, the avocado disappeared from the plate, transformed into new life.

The second half of dinner always gave way to play. María's fork began to draw shapes in the air. Her left leg swung to and fro. Her left hand reached out to pat the dog waiting patiently beside the table. Suddenly a shower of Spanish words would pour out of her mouth—the beginning of another story. This time it was something about a *rueda,* a lot of people, commotion, violence, death. Muerta, muerta, muerta—I knew that word like my own name by now.

María was talking fast and gesturing wildly. Not wanting to move my eyes from her, I started nodding, prodding her on, reaching for the dictionary which I always kept at hand, fingering automatically back toward the first half—Spanish to English. María's gestures indicated a circle, something big and obviously round. I began to look up a few words while continuing to encourage her.

She stopped. "No comprendes."

"Oh, yes I do, yes I do understand, María. You're talking about a circle. It moves. It's high but on the ground. You're telling me about your mother. You're telling me how she died." I gestured with my hands and used the Spanish words: "tu madre, muerta, la rueda." I made more hand and head gestures. "Oh yes, I do understand. La rueda. She was under it and she died." I nodded my head and raised my eyebrows: "Isn't that so?"

"No! No! No!" she cried. "¡No comprendes! ¡Máquina! ¡Una máquina! ¡No comprendes!"

María stopped and heaved a deep sigh. Then she ran through the entire story again. Still I understood only fragments. I looked desperately through the dictionary for the words on which the meaning seemed to hinge. Then she told the story for a third time, and I stared at her as she raced through it once more. Three times I had heard the same words and the same intonation. I saw the same frightened eyes and the circles in the air, felt the same intensity and seriousness; the commotion, violence, death. Muerta, muerta, muerta. Three times I couldn't understand it any better. I was desperate lest this be the only time she would tell me. If I didn't understand, I would lose her trust and she would keep it to herself forever. Muerta—locked inside forever.

"Wait, María, wait," I said, trying with my eyes to assure her of my intentions. "You're right, I didn't understand it. But wait for a few minutes. Wait till I look up a couple of words in this silly dictionary for silly gringas who don't understand." She sighed again, sat back in her chair, watched me and waited. Clearly, it was important to her. I flipped the pages as fast as I could—word, word. If it wasn't rueda— which simply means wheel, which she rejected—maybe it was rada, or just reda, I said to myself. The type was so small in this book; I realized I couldn't put it off any longer, I had to get reading glasses. María continued to pet the dog but kept her eyes glued to mine. Word, word—but I couldn't find that one word.

"Say it again, María, that one word. Rueda?—you say it wasn't really a wheel. Well, is it rada, or reda?" She said it again, loud and clear—"rueda." Maybe she was pronouncing it in a dialect, I thought to myself, or the spelling was different from the sound. No luck, I couldn't find anything but the word for wheel. María was so patient, I couldn't keep her sitting there all night. She wanted me to know how her mother died, but I couldn't find the word. I understood only the commotion, the violence, and the death. Muerta, muerta. She was lying there dead. Muerta.

"No! No!" María shook her head in exasperation. "No comprendes. Like car, four. Four on each point—like this, but big and for play. And mi mamá y mi tía y otros. They all up there"—she pointed to the ceiling. "And I waiting and waiting. That's all. And mi mamá fall down. Big red, here, very big and bloody"—she pointed to her chest. "She fall down and die. That's all. Like here, for play, we saw from car. Remember the big one, we saw from car?"

"What! María! Your mother fell off a Ferris wheel? Like the one we saw from the car?"

"Yes, see, that's all. It was—what you call?—ferawheel," she said, shrugging her shoulders and picking up Rosita, patting the doll and holding her tight as she walked across the room toward her toy box. "Let's stop. I'm tired. Let's play. Tú no comprendes anyway. Maybe someday tú comprendes. I'm tired. I'm going to color."

"María, where did you learn how to make fried bananas?" I asked as we prepared dinner in the kitchen a few weeks later. "And the salads? Did your mother teach you how to make the little salad and the big salad?"

"No, we do it together. No, she don't teach me. We just do it together."

María began to hum and sing while she cut the vegetables. Her entire body, in tune with the rhythm of scrubbing, scraping, and chopping, remembered another, earlier, happier time.

"You know, Mamá, I like making the dinner with you and going to shopping. But most of all I like to clean. That's what I want when I am older. I want to clean houses to sparkle and be very shiny and nice. On the Saturdays very early my mother like to slap!—then on my bottom I know wake up! get up! Oh I was still dreaming and sleepy. But quick, we ate the breakfast, and we swept very hard the dirt from the house with our broom. Out, out flew the dust and all the little stones, too. Most of the Saturdays our father stayed home with my brothers, and my sister and I went to the mercado with our mother. My tías and some of my girl cousins went, too. Down, down we went in the dust and the sun with the baskets, and I liked so much to follow my mother's green skirt, or the orange.

"Mamá, maybe after I learn the English I can work and bring the money to help you. That's what my mother's sisters and her brothers did for my grandmother. They worked up in the caña and the coffee, and they brought the money to her. But cleaning the houses is not so hard work, it's much better. Maybe I can work in a month or a year, after I finish the English. Then you don't have to work so much. Then we can live and play together, for always. I don't want mens. My mother say the mens drink and make babies. And the bad mens kill some of the times. I don't want the mens. I only want to be with you. Well, maybe a little sister or brother I can help take care of and play with."

"María, that song about Candi you were singing—that sounded like your mother's name. Did you learn that song from your mother?"

"No, my mother don't sing like that. I hear it at orfanato. You know, from TV. It was a cartoon about Candi, a very, very pretty little girl. She was more rubia than you, almost white hair. She had pretty little dresses, pink ones, and she sing the song on TV."

"Wasn't it a cartoon about Heidi you watched at the orphanage?"

"The song about Candi is a little like the song about Heidi, but not the same. The Heidi cartoon was an otra one— Máma, I tell you before. Heidi was morena like me, pero Candi was rubia, almost white hair. Mamá, why you always ask me the things? Why you forget when I tell you? I always have to tell you again. You don't listen to me."

The next day I parked the car at the supermarket, listening to the end of another of María's stories about her mother—a steady stream of run-on Spanish sentences of which I understood only a word here and there. "María, say it again more clearly," I turned to her when she had finished: "Was your mother's name Cándida, or Cándia?"

"Yes, it was both," she answered. "Some people call her Cande. She was so pretty, but not so dark like me. She was more white, but not so white like you. My father was more brown, and a little fat because he drink too much. You look a little like my mother, only more white—and different color hair, and blue eyes. You know, I am scared of the blue eyes, they are so light. I like the color, but I don't know why the eyes scaring me so much. Not your eyes, they have the little brown spots in them. You have a brown point on your cheek like my mother, and the little holes in your face. My father had the holes, too."

I smiled and stroked her hair. "Well, what do you say? Shall we hurry and buy something good for dinner? I'm starved, aren't you?" We opened the doors and got out of the car. I took María's hand, and she tugged at my arm, skipping and jumping over imaginary obstacles as we crossed the parking lot.

"You know why I like going so much to shopping? Because you are like my mother. Sometime she come home from work—not from an office like you but from the coffee plants—and she say: "'¡Vámanos, Jesús, al mercado!' You hear it? That's how she say it—'¡Vámanos, Jesús, al mercado!'— almost like sing. Then we walk on the road, just the two of us. We go shopping for food, like you and I, and we are happy."

In the supermarket María piled vegetables and fruits into the cart. "Here some salad, here carrots, here bananas. Can we have mangos? Maybe not so expensive today? Can we have oranges?"

"Oh sure, let's get all of them," I said. "Why don't you pick them out. And let's not forget the lemons and grapes. And look over here—tomatoes!"

"Mamá," began María as we selected the fruits and vege-

tables and put them into the cart, "I like it shopping here better because we never see the police or the Guardias. Once
when I was at the mercado with my mother we have to run
away fast because the Guardias are angry. They standing in
the middle of the street and watching us. They checking all
the people except the ones who run away. And in the trucks
they put in the people and take them. Then we hurry to the
green place—like we go to play on the swings. We are afraid,
we see the Guardias are forcing the women and girls. But we
don't stay there. We run home. We run very fast and there we
hided. No, my mother don't say something. No anything. No,
I don't remember. No anything. Anything."

María and I were silent as we put the rest of the fruit into
the cart. I reached over to pick out parsley, broccoli, and a few
potatoes.

We walked down the last aisle toward the cash registers.
Why did so many blacks pushing their carts down the aisles
seem to be smiling at me? Why did the black cashiers seem to
take special interest in María? "Hi there, you sweet thing,"
said the cashier today. "My, aren't you pretty! I guess your
mom is real happy to have such a good helper, taking those
things out of the cart for her. I know I'd sure be glad to have a
helper like you."

María gazed in reserved silence, and sighed. But the
cashier knew—"Why, that girl's smiling inside!"

In the evenings, María and I often played jacks on the floor of her room—a game at 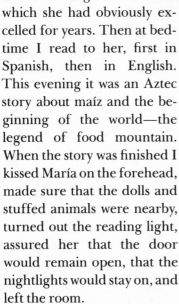 which she had obviously excelled for years. Then at bedtime I read to her, first in Spanish, then in English. This evening it was an Aztec story about maíz and the beginning of the world—the legend of food mountain. When the story was finished I kissed María on the forehead, made sure that the dolls and stuffed animals were nearby, turned out the reading light, assured her that the door would remain open, that the nightlights would stay on, and left the room.

But it was no use. María never asked for a glass of water or complained of the threatening shadows in her room. She just tried, as she had tried for a year in the orphanage, to close her eyes each night. But each night against the screen of her eyelids she reencountered in vivid detail the dark shapes of the old terrors and fears. Only the perspiration that soaked her head and her occasional attempts at language bore witness to her ongoing struggle. This again was such a night.

I heard María call "Mamá! Mamá!" and by the time I reached her room she was motioning wildly with her hands, speaking rapidly, mostly in Spanish. Sitting straight up in bed, totally awake, talking a mile a minute, she was telling another story. I kept my eyes fixed on hers as she talked, nodding automatically as she hesitated for a moment. Just as quickly, she started up again. The story was about people way up somewhere in the mountains. Sometimes they were running up, sometimes they were walking slowly and carefully. It was so pretty there—so very pretty, she repeated. The trees, the fruits, the flowers, the sun. All of it was so pretty, so nice.

Suddenly it was night. It was very dark, dangerous and scary. People were quiet, tiptoeing, whispering. Then— whoop! There were men with bandannas, with masks, carrying guns and knives.

"Who is there? What is happening?" I asked quietly.

No answer. María ignored me, as if in a trance.

This was no dream. The dreams were different, and they came in the morning. María was very conscious of relating her dreams—it was a morning ritual she knew from her life in El Salvador. So, whenever she awakened from a dream, she told me each and every image she saw, very slowly, step by step, carefully picking her words so that I would understand.

Nor was this the usual daytime story. During the day she would pick any occasion—shopping at the supermarket, walking down the street, going through the car wash—and something would trigger her memory. As if out of nowhere, she would begin in midsentence about the past. The past of the daytime stories was joyful, or painful, but it was always quite past. Nor was María entirely alone—there was an other, a listener, witnessing the articulation of the past, the making of history.

But with the nighttime stories María would begin to race and lose all sense of where she was, as if she were back in that time and reliving it. No, the nighttime stories were not yet past. They were the terror of the past that lived on in the present, frozen in María's time and in history.

After a year of silence in the orphanage, all this must have been like therapy, or confession. I was the listener, the helper, the witness. But I was a helper without hands. I was a priest who didn't know the scriptures, a therapist who had never read Freud. One night, just before I turned out the light, I listed the "fun" things we would do the next day. "All right," María sighed, turning her face to the pillow, "if I'm still alive and wake up in the morning."

Now it was already past ten o'clock. María had been talking for a half hour without stopping, except to move to the floor where I had joined her. She had told me about the people stalking, spying, walking carefully through the woods, afraid that someone would see them from behind, afraid of what they would see before them. Now I had become part of the story and had to be careful to keep my head down. We sat very close to each other so that she could whisper to me.

"Oh, oh, head down, be careful, be quiet. Oh, oh. And then, quick, the other ones, come." Now we had arrived. "Come, come. We are here." She waved her right hand to signal the ones behind her to come. "Oh, oh, look, look." María looked long and hard. I looked. "Oh, oh, todos. It is terrible," she whispered in my ear. "Todos muertos, todos," she whispered hoarsely. She paused to swallow three times. Then she was off with hardly a breath. "Todos. Todos lying on the ground"—she showed me with a sweep of her hand. "Todos"—she showed me with her finger how their throats were slashed. "Todos"—she showed me on the parts of my body how they were covered by blood. "Todos—hombres, mujeres, niños. Oh, oh, oh"—she rocked her head in her hands and made soft whining sounds.

I knew enough not to interrupt. I knew not to ask who

was where, who was found, who was running, or where it was, and where her father and mother were. I had ceased to ask questions like these during her nightly stories because once she was interrupted she stopped and shut down altogether. So I nodded repeatedly to reassure her that I was listening, trying to piece together the images and the words in my mind. This one tonight was a new story, but in all the night-time stories there was blood—death and blood.

In the orphanage, María had been asked about her family, but her elder brother had warned her not to talk. Telling what she had seen was too dangerous—she knew this from experience. Besides, she had stopped talking several years earlier, when the violence had begun. Now she felt that she could start to talk, but I couldn't understand her Spanish well enough. At first I tried to have her talk to people who were fluent in Spanish, but she refused to tell anyone else about her past. We were thousands of miles removed from El Salvador, and I figured it must have been more than a year since most of her family members had died. At that point I didn't know where they had died, or how they died, or why. I didn't even know where or how they had lived. I had read books and considered myself informed about El Salvador, but about my own daughter's history I didn't understand a thing. Only I feared that if I didn't understand, she would give up on me and stop talking. I was afraid that if I didn't remember what she had said early on, maybe we would both forget. And if we forgot, what would happen to us? What kind of people would we be?

When I contacted Doris and Ralph to ask about the boys, they told me that the children needed to play and be happy; that was the best therapy. They said that the boys—their names were now Ralph Jr. and Jimmy—were doing very well. They had each other, and no, they didn't ask about María.

The Novaks said that, for their part, they chose to look at the good side of all this. After all, we had saved the children; I should think of that. What would have happened to them otherwise? They could have died of hunger, or in the war, or of some kind of disease. I should consider the good life they now had in America. That was a lot more than their family ever had, the Novaks assured me, and the children's parents, God bless them, would be happy if they knew. I should "lighten up" and not linger on the past. Of course the boys did talk about some terrible things, the Novaks admitted, but they believed that children got over things really fast—they bounced right back.

Sometimes I doubted myself, and María. I wondered, especially after a series of sleepless nights, if I wasn't making too much of all this. Everyone seemed to be telling me not to dwell on it—it was enough to make one go mad. After all, children were known to have incredible imaginations, and how was I to separate imagination from fact? How could I be sure of anything, if she rattled on in Spanish and I hardly understood a thing? After all, if I kept running back into her room, night after night, perhaps I was the fool. Better that I should acquire good parenting skills.

Besides, I told myself, we couldn't live in the past. I had gone to El Salvador to adopt María, and now we were back in the States. I couldn't let my life be disrupted like this. I knew that children want to relate to their immediate cultural environment and fit in. We couldn't keep looking at the past and dwelling on the dark side of things. What would happen to her social adjustment? Surely in a few months these traumatic memories would pass and María would put them behind her. After all, children were supposed to be resilient.

Friends suggested that my problem might simply be the adjustment to a new person and a new way of life. Parents with newborn children were known to feel disoriented and exhausted. It wasn't all hormonal—fathers apparently felt it, too. Besides, with an adoption things tended to be more difficult, especially with an older child. All adopted children experienced trauma, and in that sense she might not have been so different. Let's face facts, I tried to reassure myself, adopted or not, all children had problems. Some children were physically handicapped, some were abused. Even when the situation was extreme, one had to keep things in perspective. After all, the idyllic childhood was a myth.

But somewhere inside myself I understood what María was telling me. I understood the stories, and I believed they were true. But I just didn't want to hear any more, and I didn't want to understand what I heard. What would I do with her stories? How would I speak? If I knew her truth, how would I continue to live with it in the world? Could I communicate what I knew? What words would I use? People would think she had made it up, or that she had seen it on television. After all, she had watched television in the orphanage. She had watched cartoons, even "Star Trek." I would have had to admit that she watched television, and that admission alone would have allowed a judge to close the case. Besides, the lawyer for the defense would claim that she imagined it, or that she simply wanted to stay up for another bedtime story or to play jacks.

Why should people believe María? Why should they believe me? Many people didn't believe what they read in news reports about El Salvador—why should they believe a child? They didn't believe what they saw on the screen night after night, right before their eyes—why should they believe me? If people didn't have a vested interest, they didn't believe what they saw. Many people didn't believe the reports about Vietnam twenty-five years earlier, and they didn't believe the

Vietnam veterans now. They seemed to prefer having them locked up in hospitals and welfare programs. If people had trouble believing their own brothers and sons, why should they have believed me? The truth is too disturbing. It disorients us and makes us tired. The people I worked with would rather not have heard about it. My friends were as busy as I was, and they became even more exhausted when I began to talk. The people who loved me were worried and wanted to put my mind to rest. Perhaps there were some who did believe me and wanted to help, but what could they do? I didn't know what to do either, so what could they do? We all keep doing what we do. But no one else heard the stories night after night. No one else lived with the dead every minute of the day.

But it was not only the dead. It was what was once connected and now was broken, violently broken. I knew that my daughter was not only herself, not only María de Jesús. She was all the things that her parents were; and their parents, and theirs. She was the people from her village. She was the countryside where they gathered their food and washed their clothes. She was the flowers and grasses, the mountains and rivers she had known. She was the images and the stories. All that lived on in her, even when everyone else was gone. I knew that she would change, but somewhere in her the past would become lodged. Somehow, I knew, all of it would live on.

Suddenly María's voice speeded up. "Quick, quick. Run away, run down the hill, down, down, quick. Nosotros, nosotros," she panted. "Quick, nosotros." She indicated with her hands and feet how we ran very fast down the hill. At the bottom of the hill there was much confusion, hands waving, argument, great urgency. We hurried, took things, wrapped them up. "Don't cry," she put her hand over her mouth. "Just

quick, quiet, shhh, shhh, quiet. Ooh, shhh. Mamá. Mamá."
Where was her mother? I told myself I shouldn't interrupt.
Anyhow, we had to be quiet. She told us firmly to be calm,
quiet. But María was slowing down. We were quiet, quiet.
Then she stopped. "Oh, oh, tengo sueño," she said, rubbing
her eyes, and I knew the story had ended. The clock indicated 11:15 P.M.

We were silent for a few minutes. María looked blankly
around the room and I stroked her head.

"Juguemos!" she cried all of a sudden, opening her eyes
wide. "Let's play jacks!"

"Well, all right," I said in a reluctant voice, reaching for
the red cardboard box of jacks on her bedside table. "Just this
once—it's already quite late." And so we ended yet another
day playing jacks on María's bedroom floor. It was the univer-
sal children's street game, at which she excelled and I was all
butterfingers.

First day of school, riddle of the morning:

"Mamá, do you think the Guardias like it when they kill the people?"

"I don't know, María."

"I think yes. Why else they do it?"

First day of school, riddle of the evening:

"Mamá, why are we in this world, if we kill each other?"

~~~~~~~~~~~~~~~~~

On her first day at school, María stood next to the teacher at the front of the first-grade classroom. She stood as she had when I first saw her in the foyer of the orphanage— head down, back straight and rigid, feet together like a soldier. But today she held no platinum-haired Rosita tightly against her chest; there were only vast, unpredictable pockets of air between herself and the strangers around her.

"María is from a country called El Salvador," the teacher said to the children, pointing to Central America on a map. "That's why she speaks Spanish and doesn't know much English yet. But we'll all help her to learn, won't we?"

In unison, the children cried, "Yes!"

"María will be with us from now on," continued the teacher, "and I hope that you will become her friends."

Then the teacher asked the children if they had any questions of María.

"Is that your mother over there?" asked a girl in the back, pointing at me in the corner.

"No," said María.

"Then where's your mother?" asked one of the boys.

"In Salvador," said María.

"Why isn't she here?" he wanted to know.

"Muerta." The teacher translated—"She is dead."

"Do you have a father?" another child asked.

"Sí."

"Where's he?"

Silence.

"Is he dead, too?"

"Sí."

The teacher bent to put her arm around María: "But now María has a new mother who loves her, and she has a home in America and many nice things. Very soon she'll have friends, too. María, aren't you glad about that?"

No answer.

The teacher squatted beside María and tried again: "Don't you think your mother and father would be happy to know that their little María is not alone any more, that she has someone who loves her very much, and soon she'll have friends to play with?"

María paused for a moment. Slowly she nodded. Yes.

"I think so, too," nodded the teacher, visibly relieved.

María looked at her for a long time. Then she added, in Spanish: "But it's not right this way."

~~~~~~~~~~~~~

It was only in the second month of her increased silence toward her young classmates about her past in remote, bloody

El Salvador that I understood how generous was María's heart. "You know, Mamá," she remarked one day after she jumped off the swing and we left the school playground: "I think the children don't still understand."

CHAPTER

21

"I think my mother is glad she is dead," said María as we sat on the floor of her room on the evening of Mother's Day, our legs stretched flat, our backs up against the side of her bed.

"There was too much moving and too much dying, too much being scared all by herself with the children. And for her last baby—it was, you know, Ramón—her milk was dried up. I remember a time. We went to the river. We washed the clothes. We washed ourselves and we went swimming. My mother sang a little and we were happy. But that was not much at the end."

The next morning I was awakened while it was still dark. There was a tug at the sheets. Someone was standing at the foot of my bed. It was María, standing like a soldier, watching me. Gradually I was able to make out the shape of her face.

"Mamá, please wake up. I had otra bad dream. This time about you."

I pushed myself up into a sitting position against the pillow and patted the mattress, signaling to María to sit beside me. She pushed up against my arm and began relating her dream, slowly and with checked breath, as always. "There was a big place, like where is fiesta. You were going someplace, otra people,

too. I want to go with you, but I can't. But otra people go. I
wait outside and want to be with you. And I wait."

María stopped and sighed. Slowly, she continued.

"I don't know anything, but I wait. Then you come out,
and something big and blood was coming out from your
dress. I think you died. I didn't want you to die. I don't
want you to die. My mother tell me when you dream it is
true. Maybe because you smoke you will die. Or because
of bad mens. Maybe here are the guns and police and the
Guardias."

María was silent. We watched the gray shapes emerge in
the morning twilight of the room. "No, María," I said after a
while. "This was a bad dream. You and I are going to be together for a long time. I am not going to die the way your
mother died. You and I will live for a long time."

"And play," said María. "You don't like play so much. You
are always working."

"Yes, María, you are going to help me play. We will play
more. We will both live and play for a long time."

After a while we stood up and went to the dresser. I
pulled out the elastic bands from María's short ponytails and
began to brush her hair. It was dark and shiny, down to her
shoulders already.

María stared at her face in the mirror, then stared at
mine, one head, chest, and set of shoulders directly above
hers. When I had finished brushing her hair and made new
ponytails, she turned away from the mirror and said,

"I am not sure of my mother's face. I am not sure in my
head for a while. I am not sure anymore in my heart. When I
was in my bed in the orfanato, I could see her face always, in
the dark in the night. I once saw a picture. She looked very
pretty. It was, you know, before she died. My sister kept the
picture and she must have it. Or if she is dead it's maybe with

somebody else. But I have no picture. How will I remember?"

"Turn around. Look in the mirror," I said. "Close your eyes. You will remember her."

"When I was very lit- tle, I like to run away from my mother when she called me to come. If she called me again and she had to run after me, she was angry. But still I like to run fast in the other direction. Miguel told me, if you run away from your mother the ground opens up a big hole. You fall in, and the earth closes the hole right over you with the dirt and swallows you up. So I was scared to run away all the time from my mother, but still some of the times I forgot and I ran any-way. Then I was scared of my father. When we were just a little bad our mother gave us a slap on our bottoms, but if we were very bad we had to wait and our father hit us with a long stick from a tree. He could bend it, and it whistled when it hit our bottoms. So when we were very bad we were scared of our father's long stick."

It was Friday afternoon, midsummer, and friends had invited us to go camping. On our drive out of town, María had been entertaining me with Salvadoran children's songs and with stories about her family and their life be-fore the war. Her earliest sto-ries had focused on her mother, but now she told me more about her father.

"For a long time my fa-ther's beard was bushy and scratchy, but not as rough as one day when he just decided and cut it. I watched him pull down sharp with the razor, but around his mouth he was careful because he had a big mustache, and he liked it. But he didn't like it if the hairs got too long on his mustache, so sometimes he cut with the scissors, snip, snip. Later most days, not every day but for sure Saturdays, my father pulled down very hard on his face with the razor.

"I liked it so much when I was running fast outside our house. Then my father catched me with his arms and threw me high in the air. Like a bird, I held out my arms and he helped me to fly. My father was always funny and happy. He liked to talk a lot, and he said many good things all of the times. That's why everybody wanted to be with our father. They came to see him and liked him so much.

"But some of the times my father was unhappy. His voice was sad and his mouth fall down and his eyes were sleepy. Then I followed him to go to the hammock, and he lifted me up to sit on top of his belly. But I didn't stay there. Sometimes I liked to crawl up even to his head to be his little flea and take out the hairs that were making him sad. Oh I always found the little white hairs hiding carefully in the forest of dark ones. I could find them and be his little flea and pick them out better and without hurting more than anybody else. Sometimes my father closed his eyes and was snoring, and his little flea was careful to stay very quiet up there, to look even in back of his ear, but carefully and so quiet. Oh I watched and picked out all the little white hairs I could find in the forest. Then I knew my father was smiling again, because his little flea kept him from being so sad."

I asked María what her father did on the days he didn't work in the fields. Did he stay at home most of the time? Did he talk a lot with the other men? What kinds of things did the men do together? I knew that the entire countryside had become politicized since the mid-1970s and that most of the campesinos had joined peasant organizations demanding more rights and better working conditions. María must have been aware, must have heard about many of these things. After all, she was probably at least seven years old when her parents died. Campesino children in El Salvador are said to understand more about politics at that age than many adults know in the States. But in her conversations with me María carefully avoided any hint of political opinion or commentary. Typically, today, she paid close attention to my questions, then, after a pause, began:

"The other mens hit the womens when they were drunk, but my father never hit my mother. My mother said, if he ever tried she would leave him. Sometimes my father got drunk with my grandfather and the others when they finished their work and got paid with the money. Then he came home drunk and talked very stupid. But my mother grabbed us and made us go out. 'No, no, stay here with me,' he said, but my mother said, 'No!' She was so angry! Then she took us to our grandmother's house up over there near the sand and the red desert. My mother's sisters and brothers lived up there with my grandmother, and I had the cousins there, too. It was so nice, we had fun, but my mother was still worried about my father. Sometimes she left us there and went down to make sure my father didn't do anything even more stupid.

"My uncles up there—you know, my mother's twin brothers—they liked to throw me up in the air like my father. They wore big boots, and they were skinny and had dark curly hair. I was a little bit scared of them because, you know, they were not like my father. He was strong and had muscles so big, but not so skinny and tall like my uncles. My mother's youngest sister was maybe twelve, maybe the same age as Miguel. She liked to take me out to bring me good fruits from the trees. I slept with her at night, or with my grandmother, because Aurelio and Ramón were wanting to be with our mother when she was there. In the morning, our mother brought us back down to our father. He was already waiting for us and happy to see us—and so sorry. My mother sometimes stayed angry and quiet for a little time more, but we were all happy to see our father again. Some of the times when she was angry I heard my mother tell Marta, 'Don't get married very soon. Men like the two things, they drink and make babies.'"

We arrived at the campground shortly before dark. Teenage boys were batting baseballs on a small field. Younger children were swinging on swings and climbing on jungle gyms in an adjacent playground. My friends had set up several tents around a campfire and were busy preparing dinner. As I stepped out of the car, my senses responded immediately to the familiar mix of fresh water, clear air, pine trees, charcoal, and grilled food. Exhausted from the day, the stories, and the long drive, I looked forward to relaxing for a weekend outdoors with friends.

But to no avail. For the next hour María refused to get out of the car. At first I tried to reassure her, pleaded with her, cajoled her, bargained with her. It was no use; she wouldn't budge. Then my friends tried one by one to persuade her to come out, but she had quickly locked her door and rolled up the window at the sight of the first approaching adult. She stared straight ahead at the dashboard, unmoved by playful winks, smiles, and entreaties. Then the adults sent their children to peer through the car window, offering María servings of hot dogs and potato salad on paper plates soaked with ketchup, mustard, and mayonnaise.

Finally I got into the car and promised María that we would return home. It was already dark, and by this time I understood that she was terrified of being in the woods during the night. I did persuade her to come with me to the campfire for a few minutes and sit on my lap and eat. Just as we had finished eating I saw a flash—someone had taken a picture of us.

As I turned the key in the ignition and started down the dark winding road through the state park, I listened to the strains of an old Woody Guthrie ballad somebody had struck up as we left. Why had I been so naive as to try to go camping with María? I thought to myself. Why had I been stupid enough to drive two and a half hours to the campground? Why did it all have to be like this?

During the ride through the park and a longer one on a desolate county road, María didn't say a word to me, but stared straight ahead, ignoring my attempts at conversation. She sat rigid in the passenger seat, the perspiration still visible on her forehead—from anger and fear, not from the heat. For half of the trip home she maintained her sullen silence, but as we approached a highway with glaring lights and billboards, she suddenly brought forth a string of opinions and instructions in a harsh, clipped tone that I'd never heard from her:

"I don't want to be with other peoples. I just want to be with you. I don't want to sleep outside at night. It's crazy to do when people have nice beds in their houses. I don't want to be in a tent in a smelly sleeping bag with other childrens like you told me. I want to be in my room in my own bed. I lived outside my whole life. We cooked outside and we ate outside. I never thought it was bad, I liked it. I never knowed anything else. But it's better in a house, especially when it's not so warm, and almost raining like now. I don't want to play with other childrens in tents, in the dark. I don't want you to do it either, with womens and mens. I just want to stay at home. People go out too much. There is too much troubles. I want us just to stay home and be happy. Just you and me."

I was too astonished at this outburst to say anything except to apologize quietly and say she was right. Then María perked up and in a high, clear voice began to sing all the children's songs she knew from El Salvador—about dolls, toys, birds, games, and some little girl from China. La Chinita, she was called, that was obvious.

It was already after midnight, and we still had another hour to go. Exhausted, I tried to concentrate on my driving and ward off the resentment that was creeping up on me—the feeling of being trapped, smothered. At one point it occurred to me that my friends would still be sitting around the campfire, drinking wine, talking and joking about familiar things, their children fast asleep in a separate tent in those smelly sleeping bags. All of a sudden I felt like screaming at María, but I didn't. I only felt trapped, utterly alone.

In the photograph taken of us that night at the campfire, our bodies looked very soft and a bit swollen around the edges. Perhaps it was because the picture was shot with a Polaroid camera. We were both dressed in shorts, our skin giving off a pastel pallor, almost a glow. María was sitting on my lap, her head tucked under my chin, her legs draped over mine and seeming too long because of the camera angle. The background was dark, almost black, and we were looking with resigned weariness into the remains of a campfire. I was hardly the Madonna in the great armchair. I seemed small and vulnerable in a way I had never thought of myself, hardly bearing up under María's weight. Her face had an ancient, mournful look. I appeared strangely younger, more frightened.

CHAPTER

23

Gradually I tried to reconnect with the world outside on a more regular basis. At first, I would go out for a couple of hours, to dinner or to a movie with a friend. María would usually make her loudest protests as I put on lipstick in front of the mirror, saying she knew exactly where I was going and what I was planning to do.

"You are dressed pretty. You are painting your face, going to be with mens. I know. I know what you are going to do with mens." She would show me what she meant by jerking and rotating her hips, then suddenly turn beet red and slap her hand over her mouth.

The preparation for one of these evenings would wear me out emotionally, and it would take me days to recover. Usually I would return at about 11 P.M. María was inevitably still awake. According to the babysitter, she would spend the entire evening next to her bedroom window, listening for my step on the front walk. The babysitter was always friendly and polite, but from the strained expression on her face I would know that María had taken out my absence on her. After a while, the bewildered teenager would reluctantly admit to me that María had not spoken one word for the entire evening. Indeed, María's most effective weapon was her silence.

~~~~~~~~~~~~~~~

"*It was one of the Saturdays* and our mother made us the beans, they were hot. Marta was sitting next to me. She had on the pretty yellow dress she wore to the parties, because when there was dancing my parents took her to the parties—you know, to protect. All the boys like Marta so much! She was so pretty! But really I think they like any girl if she was a girl, because when the girls were walking together the boys raised their eyebrows at all the girls and looked at them strong.

"Anyway, Marta and our father argued for a long time about something. I remember I didn't look up. I was looking straight at the beans and waiting for them not to be hot. My mother told me to watch, they were hot. I couldn't see the hot anymore, but I knew they were hot, still too hot. All of a sudden next to me Marta was shaking and mad and stood up. Even if they were not boiling, still for a little girl the beans were too hot. It happened so fast, and probably Marta didn't mean it at all. Or she was excited and her arm just forgot. Anyway, all of a sudden the beans fell on me and burned me a little. My mother wiped me and cleaned me. She put something on the place that was burning, and she said it was nobody's fault. I know Marta didn't at all mean it. Never mind, our father was angry. He didn't talk loud, but still you could see he was angry. Marta forgot, she didn't mean it, but our father got up and took off his belt and hit Marta. If we little ones were bad and our mother told our father, he hit us with the stick from the tree. But when Marta or Miguel did something very bad he took off his belt. But really, Marta didn't mean it at all. Anyway, that was the day Marta left us. It was many, many days before she ever came back.

"Marta worked for a long time picking the coffee up there in El Chile. It was a good job and she liked it, because the coffee was much better than working and sweating so hard in the caña. Marta had long hair, but she wasn't so tall and quiet like our mother. She was small and a little bit round like our father, and she was happy and funny a lot—except for that day when she was so unhappy and angry. But when she came back to us—oh, oh, Marta! Her hair was cut very short to her shoulders, and she had a big belly! The hair and the belly were not the same anymore, but everything else was still Marta. Then she showed us her husband. He was thin with a beard and he wore glasses. Maybe our father didn't like Marta's husband so much, but later he went in back of our house and they built together a little straw house for Marta and the new baby."

"I don't want mens," María protested every time someone came over or I went out. "Womens are all right. Some womens. But no mens. Mens are bad. They rape womens and kill babies. I know it. I saw it. The mens kill each other, too. You like that? You want me to like that?"

"No. I believe you, and I understand what you're telling me," I would reply. "But not all men do what you've seen. Many men are good. Think of Robert, or Thom, or Skip. You've told me you like them. Not all men do the bad things you've seen."

I didn't want to imply that she should simply forget the past, or that things here were entirely different. I didn't want to lie. We didn't have government security forces and death squads massacring citizens; instead we sold our armaments to other countries and looked away when they were used. I didn't want to imply that she was safe from violence in this country. We had a big black dog, half Doberman, half German shepherd, and our dog wasn't there to protect us from the women in our neighborhood. I didn't want to lie.

"You told me your father was a good man," I said to María, "and you have three brothers. You told me you love your brothers very much."

"Yes," she replied, "but that was my father, and they are my brothers. My father never hit my mother, but the other mens hit the womens. My father's father, my grandfather, did it, and my tías' husbands did it, too. Maybe it's not so bad like what the army soldados do when they rape and kill the womens. But if they're your wife and you love them and you hit the womens, it still hurts the womens. I saw how my tías cried when they were hit. I know, it hurts very much."

"Yes," I said. "Men in this country hit their wives, too. Not all men. But some men do it. And here men rape women, too. But we have laws and women are more protected here. When the woman talks about it, the man is punished. These things are bad and the men who do them should be punished. But that doesn't mean that men are bad inside. They do bad things because bad things happen to them, sometimes when they're very little. Maybe nobody takes care of them, or somebody hits them a lot. Boys are told they should be big and strong and not have many soft feelings to show. So some of them get mean and wild, even when they're little."

"That's how some of my boy cousins were," María interrupted. "They acted crazy."

"And many girls," I said, "are told they should be shy and

quiet, and not make trouble at all, and only dress pretty and play with their dolls. . . ."

At this last sentence María sat straight up in her chair and glared at me, as though she'd never before considered the situation from that angle. Then she giggled and burst into gales of laughter.

"*I remember one day* after the baby was born he was coughing so much and crying. It was a sad night, so lonely, and my mother and Marta told me to stay on the bed with the sick baby. Why couldn't he stop crying? I wanted to shake him, but he was little and tiny and sick. I don't know why, but I still wanted to shake him even though I knew he was sick. Outside, everybody was sitting next to the fire and the kitchen and talking. But I was mad because I had to stay on the bed with the sick baby. Sometimes he wasn't crying so much anymore, just lying there sad, even when Marta came and wiped him and held him. The fever was bad, he was crying inside, you could see it. But after a while I started to dream and was sleepy. When I woke up in the morning, the baby didn't make the sick sounds anymore. He was dead. I kept remembering how I was angry at him and wanted to shake him to stop making the sounds. I felt very sorry. But he decided to die and now he was dead. Somebody made a box for him, one of the small ones for babies. I know they buried him somewhere with flowers. But I don't know where it was, and I don't remember his name.

"Marta and her husband stayed for a while in the little straw house. Oh we thought there was something, because we heard them. We were wondering, because when my girl cousins and I played in the trees near the little straw house, we knew they were inside. It was in the middle of the day, but we heard them. Shhh, shhh, we picked up our feet and put them down carefully. We were close to the house and sneaking, and laughing inside. Shhh, shhh, we were very close now, being so quiet and sneaking. Then we looked through the straw—it was dark, cool, and quiet. Oh we saw them! My sister and her husband were very close together, almost naked! We tried to make not even a sound, but they must have heard us, or they felt we were there. All of a sudden they stopped and turned, and they saw us. Marta laughed and told us to go. She said they were making another baby. Then we ran away very fast to the bushes, and my heart was so pounding and our faces were red."

24

It was a midsummer evening, and María had brought her colored pencils and drawing paper to the dining room table after dinner. One brown and white house after another appeared on the paper, followed by green fruit trees with orange circles on them. Standing in front of the houses were large to small stick-figure people. The large ones held a broom, a bowl, a pile of wood, or a machete. The small ones, the children, smiled at us with their arms outstretched and their legs planted firmly apart, the girls carefully distinguished from the boys by their long hair, eyelashes, and swing-out skirts with the point on either side.

"This is how we lived in San Antonio," said María after I had sat down next to her and watched for a while. "Here is the road," and she drew a long meandering line across the paper. "It went around in front of our house like this. Then it turned up the hill to the mountains and the caña, just like this. That's my mother in front of the house. I'm next to her, helping. The big house in the middle is my grandparents' house. It was the biggest, but here it looks little. See, that's my grandmother Tonia standing in front. Behind are the three steps from her house to ours. That's where I liked to climb when I was little. Over there the big leaves are the bananas next to my uncle Pablo's house. I like to run there and bring us bananas to eat. Over here the little one is the house where my father's sister Pilar lived with her husband and children. My tía Olivia and her children lived with my grandparents because her husband was gone a long time. I think they never found him.

"You see here behind our house? You see the dot? There my father built the little straw house for my sister and her baby. But I didn't draw it really, because the house wasn't there all the time. After the baby died, Marta and her husband went back to El Chile, and my father took down the straw house because we didn't need it anymore."

"How far was your other grandmother's house—your mother's mother's house?" I asked.

"We walked on the other road, up here. It was first across a big place with no trees, like a red desert. Oh but near our grandmother's house it was so nice! Fruits, so many fruits! And my grandmother like so much her maíz and her beans and her fields. There I played with her daughter, the youngest one, my mother's little sister. She was not so old—like Miguel, maybe eleven, or twelve."

"And your grandfather up there?"

"No, he was dead. I never saw him. But my mother's sisters and their children sometimes came to there. They all up there worked in the same caña with my father and the others. But my mother's younger brothers—you know, the twins, the ones tall and skinny with the curly hair—they lived with my grandmother in her house. They worked up there too in the caña and brought her the money."

"María, where is the little store—the tienda?"

"Down here, from our house. It isn't far. You can see it where the road is turning to go down to the big road, where we climbed into the truck for the market. But it was more easy just to go to the little store when we didn't need much.

Sometimes—not in the beginning, only when I was older—I liked to run there to buy things for my mother. You know, there my grandmother's friend lived with her little girl. It was her tienda. It's where my grandmother and my mother's youngest sister hided at the end, where they were all killed. The soldados found there the woman and the little girl in the tienda, and my grandmother and my mother's little sister were hiding with them. Then they brought there my mother's twin brothers, and the others. The soldados took all them in front of the pared right next to the tienda—you know, a wall is a pared. First they raped the women and the girls; then they shot all the people standing there. But here it is too far down for the paper, so I'll leave off the pared and the tienda."

"María, were you there? Did you see the people killed?"

No answer.

"Did your parents go there and see what happened? Did somebody tell them about it?"

No answer.

"María, where was the finca where everybody worked?"

"This little road turning behind our house up goes to the caña. On the other side behind our house is our maíz and our beans. See, I draw it, how big is the maíz! Sometimes when he was in a hurry, my father went on this little road straight up in the middle. It was faster. When our mother was finished cooking she called us, and we went with my cousins up this little road, too, to carry up the dinner. Up, up we ran past our beans and our maíz, up past the rows of the caña. Then we saw them! Oh it was everywhere hot and sunny, but it was so nice because we all of us sat together in the shady place under the big tree. I liked it to be sitting in the middle of my cousins and uncles and tías! And best of all, when I was sleepy, I like to crawl in the grass under my father's leg like a cool cover. There I dreamed a long time and smelled the sweet leaves."

"Was there a house, or was it all fields?"

"It was a very, very beautiful house with a swing, and a porch on all the sides went around it. But it was lonely and big all by itself in the fields. The man lived there, or near there, and he was big and fat because he ate all the food, even when the others were working. Everybody said he was bad, because he stole our money. Maybe he wasn't so bad, only greedy. Anyway, he sat and watched all day while we were working. Every day a woman brought hot food and salads, but only for him. It was enough for all of us, but he ate it all up. Oh he got paid much to watch and tell stories about us. But it wasn't real work. He used to work with my father and the others, so he knew how to cut the caña. But now he just sat in the big chair and ate salads and listened and watched.

"That was why somebody paid him, it was big money. My father and the others had to work all the long hours and didn't get very much paid—but he had a gun and ate salads. Then he made my father and the others stay one hour late every day, and he gave no time in the middle for the dinner. That was when they got mad and they left him. Good-bye, you are not nice, we won't work for you anymore, my father and the others said to the fat man. But he didn't like it. He watched with a gun, and his friends had the guns. He was scared all the time that the people wanted more money and more time to be lazy—he was scared they would trick him. But they didn't want to trick him. They only wanted not so many hours to work, and in the middle of the day they wanted the time for the dinner.

"So my father and the others were mad and they left him. Then the fat man ran after them and told them wait, wait, now I need you, I need you to work. But it was only because he was afraid about himself, he didn't care anymore about the others. So after all the lies and the watching and listening, they didn't believe him anymore, and they left. Quick, quick, my father and the others ran down the little road, and turned around and around all the bushes, and ran, down, down. And all of a sudden they were so happy, because they saw my mother and my grandmother and all us childrens standing outside our houses, waiting for them. That's when they told us they were mad and left the fat man."

"So that was the big farm, the finca, and the man must have been the foreman."

"Yes, maybe. But my father and my uncle Pablo and my grandfather and the others never went back up there again. They had to be hiding. In the nights, our mother covered us on our beds and told us to be quiet. We heard the men walking very quietly outside, and we saw how they shined their flashlights all around our houses, looking for my father and the other mens. My mother told us not to be scared, it would look bad to kill the mothers and children so soon; but after the first night, she told Miguel to sleep up there outside with the others. Oh they never found them. My father and the others knew very well the caves for hiding up in the mountains, and the men with the masks and the flashlights and the knives sneaking and looking for them were not so smart—they couldn't find them. But for a long time my father and the others had to stay outside up there in the nights. It was not so good in the caves. They liked much better to sleep at home in their own beds.

"I remember in the beginning, one of them didn't believe it. He said it wasn't serious. He said he wanted to stay right there in the night and sleep in his house with his wife and his children. The next morning somebody found his body with the throat cut lying just at the side of our houses. It was maybe my tía Pilar's husband—you know, the one who didn't believe my father and the others. He wanted just to stay in the night in his own house.

"But some of the nights, even my father was worried because my mother had the big belly again. Ramón was coming, we didn't know when. But when my mother said it was almost time, then my father didn't go in the night all the way up to the hiding place of the caves with the others. He wanted to stay near his own house in the maíz, just in case. That's how Ramón was born a little bit later. My mother was on the bed behind the black plastic, helping Ramón to come in this world and be born. It was one of those mornings when my father came back to our house from the maíz. He was cooking the chicken for my mother outside, and drinking the coffee. All of a sudden we heard the cry from the baby—it was Ramón! Oh the maíz was very tall, and my father was little and quick. If you knew what you were doing, you could hide very well in the maíz."

"María, I don't see the bench outside your house where your father liked to sit, or the hammock."

"They were here, next to the mango tree. You see the big circles, the mangos? But I forgot to draw the bench and the hammock. And I forgot the place here, where we made the fire and the dinner. There is no more room on the paper. We have to imagine. Maybe you can see it in your mind."

CHAPTER

25

"Have you ever heard of a place called San Antonio?" I asked a labor union organizer from El Salvador, a political refugee who was in sanctuary with the Quakers. We were at a potluck dinner to help raise funds for the sanctuary movement.

"I know many," Ernesto replied. "San Antonio is very popular with us, like your Williamsburg or Johnstown. How big is it?"

"I'm not sure. It must be a mountain community next to a finca or hacienda. It could be as small as a hamlet."

"Well, there are cities and towns," he said. "San Antonio Los Ranchos in the North, another San Antonio in the West near Santa Ana."

"This San Antonio must be fairly close to the city of San Vicente. On Saturdays María's family went there to market in the back of a truck."

"Yes," Ernesto smiled, "that is how the campesinos travel when they don't walk." Then, as if absentmindedly, he added: "We lived for a few years in San Vicente. I know it well. I have heard of some San Antonios around there on the volcano, but I have never been there. There were some bad massacres up there a few years ago. Afterwards, the city was full of refugees."

"Oh!" I was stunned. "Where were the massacres? Can you tell me anything

131

about the refugees? I wonder how many San Antonios there could be around a city like San Vicente."

"Who know," he smiled sadly, and shrugged. "Everything is changing so fast in our country since the civil war started. The campesinos move around from place to place, following the harvests. That has been going on for years, for over a century really, since the government took the land away from the Indians in the first place. Now the people move as the battlefronts change. One week you see a row of huts on one mountain road. The next week they are empty. The people are living in another row of huts on another hill, or they are in a refugee camp where there is even more poverty and disease. Or they are dead, and the dogs and birds eat the corpses. All this is part of the government strategy to uproot and displace the peasant population, to separate them from the armed resistance. But in the long run, the more the army intervenes forcibly, the more the peasants dig in their heels and support the popular movement and the FMLN."

"The problem is, I don't know how to connect María's story to all this," I said to Ernesto. "What I know comes from you, and others like you, and from newspapers and books. But I hear the story of María's family through the words of a child who was in the middle of it all. It is a struggle, but I am trying to bring these two parts, the two stories, together. I wish I knew where her family lived. I wish I knew more about the San Vicente volcano. If I had a good map, it would help."

"The Indian name of the volcano is Chinchontepec," Ernesto said. "In this region was the great uprising of the Indians against the landowners in the nineteenth century. The Indian leader's name was Anastasio Aquino. He was a laborer from an indigo plantation, and after he captured the city of San Vicente he crowned himself the king of the Nonualcos. After a few days the government army massacred the Indians, executed Aquino, and put his head in a cage on a hillside, for all to see. So you can understand, there is much history, many memories in this region. The campesinos pass down the stories from one generation to the next. They all know that this is not the first time it has happened, and it probably won't be the last. But look"—Ernesto's eyes brightened for a moment—"even if you find all the San Antonios on the best map, it won't matter. You have to live there to understand. Maybe you will go there one day yourself. Who knows, maybe we can all go back there one day."

I smiled at him, knowing this was his dream.

"Poor little María, poor little one," said Ernesto's wife Teresa in a mixture of Spanish and English, leaning over to put her hand on María, who had been sitting silently between us. "You didn't have anything, did you, my little one, when you came with your family down to San Vicente."

María was quiet, but her eyes said she liked hearing the familiar provincial San Vicente sounds.

"I know it. I know how terrible it was," Teresa continued. I know how bad was the fighting in that area of San Vicente where the refugees lived. I saw how the Guardias and the police treated the people. I know how they pushed them around and kicked them, how they killed the people secretly in the night."

Tears came to María's eyes, and she looked down.

"Don't worry, little one." Teresa said. "You don't have to talk about these things if you don't want to. But you can believe, I know them. Ernesto and I both know them. We still see the terrible things when we close our eyes, and we dream about them in the night. Teresa moved her face close to María's: "María, maybe you have the dreams, too?"

María kept her head down. The tears stood in her eyes.

"It will be all right," Teresa said, looking at me while she stroked María's head. "The campesino children are strong, and they understand what has happened to their families and to them. They also know that it is dangerous to talk too much. They know when it is better to hide and be quiet. Don't worry, it will be all right. It will just take kindness and patience, and some years' time."

Conversation turned to the Salvadoran dishes that Teresa and a few other Salvadoran women had prepared, and we started to eat. Engrossed in her eating, María stayed quiet, but the minute we were alone in the car on the drive home, she began to talk:

"Ernesto and Teresa look a little bit like my padrino and madrina—you know, the ones they held me up when I was a tiny baby and somebody put the water on my head. But they died, and my mother found me a new padrino and madrina when we lived in San Vicente, just in case. I think the second padrino and madrina wanted to go away to work in Estados Unidos. They had a house in San Vicente much more nicer than our house, and a little garden, and more money. And I think they had TV—it was the first time I saw TV. Anyway, our mother took us to their house after our father died, and I know she talked with the people. Then she told us if anything happened, we should go there and they would get food for us. But after she died I never saw them anymore, and they were gone from their house. Maybe they died, or maybe they went away somewhere to work. Maybe now they are in Estados Unidos, too.

"Anyway, my first padrino and madrina were my parents' good friends. They lived way up in the mountains, but sometime they come to San Antonio and visit us and talk with my mother and father. One of the times it was before the soldados were coming and we had to go away from San Antonio. I remember we took all our things from our house and jumped up in the truck. We were all of us in the back of the truck, going down the road away from our houses, and I remember I liked it always so much when the wind was strong in my hair. All of a sudden the truck stopped. Two people were lying on the side of the road, and my father and mother jumped down from the truck because they thought they knew them. They went over to them and touched them and turned them over. You could see their faces were torn away by the guns from up close. The one was shot in the nose and the other, the woman, was shot in the mouth. Their faces were gone, you couldn't see them anymore. All that was left was the pink meat behind them. They must have been hurrying down, running away from the army soldados, and the soldados must have come from behind them and surprised them. They were shot from up close and their faces were blood. Our parents knew they were their good friends, even if you couldn't see their faces at all anymore. They were my first padrino and madrina. Then my parents were sad and they jumped into the truck, because we had to hurry away fast from San Antonio and our houses."

CHAPTER

26

"After we leave San Antonio, we live with our parents in the woods more near San Vicente. We live in a house where my parents knew the family, but they were gone, maybe dead. There were many killings there, many. That was the first time I saw so many dead bodies. I was scared all the time. They were in the mornings lying on the road or beside the road, and near the houses. I think that's when I stopped being happy and stopped talking so much. After my mother died I stopped even more, that was the worst. But I think it started when we left San Antonio. We were all of us scared and more quiet.

"Near our house we were walking on the road, and we saw four bodies. On the other side of the road was a small truck with four of the army soldiers. I remember, because they had on the special wide round helmets with light stripes, like the top of a pie, crossing each other. The soldiers just were looking and driving slowly beside us in their small truck. They didn't say anything or do anything, so everybody knew who tortured and killed the four men. Later a woman came there with a truck. She tried to pick up the bodies and pull them up in the truck, because the four were her sons. Some of the other people from around there came to her and helped her. Together they pulled up the bodies in the truck, so she could take her four sons to be buried somewhere.

"One day Miguel and I were looking for sticks, because my father carried the wood to the market in San Vicente. He try to sell it to buy the maíz, so my mother could cook for us. First we thought it was a stick, but we found a bone from a dead person, and another one. Then we found many of the bones all around the house where we were living. We showed them to our mother. I remember when she looked at them she was angry and told us to drop them. It was bad luck.

"My father died one of the days soon after that. I think maybe it was Marta's husband who pushed him. They were standing in the street, and maybe they argued. They were near the gas station where were the checking points and the Guardias. They were coming back from the market with the maíz, because they sold all the wood. They must have been drinking, and maybe it was Marta's husband who pushed him. Somebody said there came a car in the street, and my father fell in the street, and the car drive by fast and it hit him. But Marta's husband didn't stay there to help him. He ran away to tell my mother, and then he ran very fast up to El Chile. I don't think Marta's husband helped my father. He just run far away. Somebody tell us the Guardias were laughing. They tell them the driver was sorry, he would pay for the box. But my father's friends who saw it were very angry. They took my father from the street in their truck and drove him to the clinic. But it was too late and my father was already dead.

"Many peoples came there very angry and sad to the party for our father. He had on the white sheet in the box, but not all the way up. On his chest you could see it was very dark and pushed down. On his face it was pushed, too, you could only see the half. I know very well, because my mother held me up and I looked close down at him in the box. I know, and when she held me up over him my mother said, 'There is your father, remember him.'

"After my father died, we were scared anymore to live in the house so far away from the big road. So we took our things to where my grandparents and tías and cousins were living in San Vicente. It was on the same road where we used to go in the truck from San Antonio to the market. Now we just walked to the market, it was more close.

"Here, I can draw it on the paper. Our house was here, and over there was the bridge over the mud river. We played on the road with my cousins when no cars were coming—my mother didn't like it. That's how we ran to go swimming in the pools, you know, where was the much caña. Here on the paper was another river, but the shoe factory up there made it smell bad and the color was orange and green. This other way was the gas station, just before we came to the checking point to go into the city. You know, that's where my father was killed. The Guardias were always standing there holding their guns strong and straight. They were very scary because they had on the uniforms with the shiny buttons and the big boots. They were checking everybody's shirts and pockets every time you had to go past them to go to the market. Here, across from the checking point, is the hospital where they took my father. But he was already dead.

"We children stayed by ourselves only one time. It was when my mother and my tías and my grandparents went to San Vicente to vote. My mother didn't want to go. It was just after my father died. Anyway, my mother was tired and sad, but you had to go. Everybody had to vote. They wanted to shoot you if you stayed home and didn't vote. But we were scared to stay by ourselves because there was shooting around us. We could hear the guns and the rockets all the day. Our mother told us we shouldn't go out but just lie down and put our hands covering our heads. There was a thick wall next to the door, and that's where our mother told us to stay. Miguel and our older cousins were not so afraid from the shooting, or they didn't show it. But some of my cousins and my little brothers and I stayed behind the wall a long time.

"One of the days I was standing in the door, looking out. I remember because my mother was sewing the tear in a skirt for me. I remember it was quiet. All of a sudden there was a bomba so loud, and the sand from where it exploded flew into my eye. It hurt me a lot, very sharp, and my mother didn't have time to help it. We all went very fast away from the door and lied on the floor. There were all kinds of bombas and shooting. The soldados from up there on the mountain were on the other side of the bridge trying to come in the city, and the army soldiers were on this side of the road trying to keep them out. I was never so scared as that time from the noise. We had to stay on the floor a long time, because sometimes the bullets came to our house. Our mother told us to crawl behind the thick wall, it was more safe. Some of the times my mother was crying and praying out loud. I don't know how long we had to be there, but I think it was one day and one night. We were very hungry. We couldn't move, and we couldn't eat anything because the kitchen was outside. We couldn't sleep either because the bombas were exploding. When we got up and came out of our house, it was a long time later. On the other side of the road people were standing around the one house. We knew the people who lived there, it was a mother and her daughter. They were lying on the floor. One bullet killed both of them, just the one. First it hit the mother in the stomach. Then it hit the daughter in the heart, she was behind her."

It was bedtime—we had been sitting at the table for almost two hours. María helped me clear the dinner dishes from the table and put them in the sink. We were silent. As we

slowly walked upstairs to her room, María continued. "Two
big dogs always waited in the mornings when we came out of
our house. The black and brown dog had its blood, and the
two came together. My mother told me not to look. I always
looked anyway because I knew what it was, and I knew the
dog was going to have the babies. The mother dog didn't have
very much milk, so soon after they came out, all the little ones
died except one. It was the one my mother wanted most to
live and she helped it. But the mother dog died a little bit later. A man with a stick liked to tease dogs. He was crazy, and
he hurt the mother dog in her private. We found her on the
road when she already smelled and was dead. My mother
wrapped the mother dog in a blanket and took her under the
bridge. Nobody buried the dogs. There were too many dead
people around to be buried, and some of the people weren't
buried either. Sometimes nobody came to get them, and they
started to smell after a while. But nobody wanted to bury
somebody if nobody came, in case somebody's family came
later looking for them. Or nobody could find them, or the
dead person's family was too scared. So sometimes other people found them when they were finished smelling and already bones. That's how it was in the house next to ours. It
was empty. It was bigger than ours, so a lot of people must
have lived there. But when some of our friends came to live
there from San Antonio, they found the bones everywhere.
They were frightened, it might be a sign, so they went to live
somewhere else. That's why nobody else came to live there
and why they called it the house of the dead. It was big and it
had lots of room for a family. But there were too many bones,
it was scary. Anyway, the dead dogs and the people lied
around many days. Then the big black birds came and they
ate them. Just the blanket stayed for the mother dog under
the bridge. But the baby dog my mother wanted most to live
stayed around us much longer."

We were driving across town to the movies to see a Disney cartoon. As we approached a busy intersection, I put the turn signal on and pulled into the left lane just as the traffic light turned red. Waiting for the light to change, I noticed María staring at the driver of the car next to us—a pretty young woman with dark curly hair. When the light turned green, the woman smiled quickly at María before our two cars sped off on their separate ways.

"Mamá, she look just like Marta!" María exclaimed as I turned the corner. "Maybe not so much the color, but for sure the way she look with her eyes."

I started, imagining how it might be if we ever encountered Marta by chance on the street. Then I placed the idea of Marta once more into the past and asked María what she had looked like.

"She was so pretty! She had the eyes sweet and the curly hair. And I like so much to watch her when she dress up to go to the parties." María was pensive for a while, then said, "You know, Mamá, I miss my sister. I think maybe I could talk to her better about some of the things. In Salvador, the girls talk to their older sister about special things, not always to the mother. They talk to their sister"—María blushed and put her hand over her mouth. "Well," she said slowly and glanced at me shyly. "You know, when they are older they can talk to them more better about their bodies."

Taken aback, I asked María if perhaps the girls could learn to feel comfortable talking to their mother if they had no older sister.

"Yes, maybe," she replied, but she was off on another tack. "Mamá, I never tell you, but after my mother died, Marta take me up with her to El Chile for a few days. We take the truck that goes a long way around and goes up. But it wasn't very good. There was more fighting up there and the planes try to throw the bombas on us. Anyway, Marta didn't stay with me so much. She had her own friends, and she had little Marinita who need her and cry for her so much. You know, all the womens up there had the mens, and Marta after her husband died she was so lonely. So I couldn't be with her in the nights. Mamá, I think about it sometimes. I think all the mens and the womens come together so much because they were very scared and so lonely up there."

"It must have been scary and lonely for everybody up there, the children, too."

"I know little Marinita was scared, even though she had Marta. But there were not so much childrens. Anyway. Marta told me she couldn't take care of me anymore. That's when she take me on the truck back to San Vicente to my tías and my grandparents and my brothers. I remember Marta was sad and cry much. She say it was too dangerous up there for the childrens, and anyway she had little Marinita who need her so much."

"It must have been very hard for Marta to take you back to San Vicente. She must have thought your grandparents and your tías and Miguel could take better care of you."

"Yes. But you know, Mamá, before our mother died I like

going so much up to El Chile. It was so high up, and all around us were oranges, oranges, oranges! I worked in the coffee, too, and I had a small basket. But most of the times I played and took care of my little brothers and Marinita. Sometimes we saw the planes and heard the shooting already when there was fighting near us."

"María, where were Marta and her husband when there was fighting?"

"They were with us, picking the coffee. One day the army soldiers came to us in the coffee and they called out four. The four were two mens and two womens, and one of them was Marta's husband. I remember Marta's husband dropped quick the basket, and he and the other man and the womens ran away very fast through the coffee trees and the maíz, and the soldiers chased them. Later some of the people went out and looked for the four. They thought they were up there, that's where they find them. It was a little road with sharp rocks and bushes, and when they looked down they saw all the four. First they saw Marta's husband because he didn't fall all the way down. He was caught in a tree, that's how they find them. The other ones falled all the way down. The throats were cut, and there was much blood. Marta's husband's throat was cut, too, but not all the way. After they brought them back to El Chile, they put the two mens and the two womens lying in front of the big house, and all the people from El Chile came there and saw how the soldiers hurt them and kill them. They were four heads and four bodies. Up close, I remember you could see Marta's husband's throat, how it was cut. But not all the way, because you could still see the small piece of meat that tied his head to his body."

"And you were there with Marta and your mother?"

"Yes, and Marinita and my brothers."

"And your father—he was already dead?"

"Yes."

"And Marta? How was Marta?"

"I don't remember until the night, she cry very much. I know my little brothers and Marinita were sleeping. I was sitting with Marta and Miguel and my mother next to the box. Marta cry to the box and her husband. 'Take me with you,' she cry, and you know in her belly she had the new baby. We sat for a long time in the dark and we watched her and heard her. Now it was louder, and again to the box, 'Take me with you.' She standed up, her belly was big, and she stretched out her hands to the box, 'Take me with you.' Then all of a sudden we saw it. All of a sudden when she cried very loud 'Take me with you' he heard it. We all saw it, he heard it. Marta was scared and stopped crying because he heard it. 'Take me with you.' The box moved a little to tell her he heard it.

"The next day they carried the four to the place for the dead at the end of El Chile. The graves were open and fresh, and the people brought flowers. I was standing near to Marta, because I remember she had the big belly. She stood close to the grave and looked down. She wanted to jump to her husband, and she cried again, 'Take me with you.' Three of them came from behind her and held her, but she pulled down to the grave and her husband. 'Take me with you, take me with you.' It was still fresh and open, she wanted to go. But the three of them from behind her held her back, and the other ones pushed the ground over the box and the husband. A little time after that day the baby was born, it was a boy. He was happy and round, but a little time later he was sick and he died from a fever."

We had reached the theater parking lot. "María, do you still want to see the movie?" I asked, overwhelmed by the story about Marta, wondering if it hadn't been too much for both of us.

"Oh yes!" she exclaimed. "I hear about the movie already from TV, about all the little cute dogs with the black spots on them. Let's go, Mamá!" she cried, jumping out of the car. "Let's hurry!"

CHAPTER

28

It was the beginning of the fall semester, and the FMLN representative had just given a lecture at the university. He cupped his hand behind his left ear and pushed his head forward across the lectern as I looked up at him and repeated the words: "Chile! A place called El Chile!" People were pushing and crowding around him— everyone wanted at least a brief word with the FMLN representative. "Chile! El Chile!" I said much louder this time. "El Chile! It's up in the mountains, somewhere around San Vicente," I heard myself shouting as he shook his head slowly. It wasn't clear whether he couldn't hear me, whether he had never heard of the place, or whether he didn't want to talk about it. "It's on the San Vicente volcano. They grow coffee—café," I said hoarsely. "I'm almost sure it's pronounced El Chile. Do you know anything about such a place?"

The FMLN representative peered at me over his glasses. "Yes," he said deliberately, and nodded. "What do you want?"

The question took me by surprise. What did I want? But of course, this man couldn't imagine what in the world I might want of him. I wanted everything—all the information, the dates, the names, and the places. I wanted to know where everybody was—the survivors, the missing, the dead.

"What do you want?" he asked once again, a bit impatiently as the people crowding around him were anxiously waiting their turn.

"Please," I said. "I only want to know if a place called El Chile really exists. I'm not sure because I can't find it on a map. I've asked many people, but no one has heard of it, and I can't find it listed in any books. I have adopted a child"—I felt ill at ease with all the people crowding around us. "Please, just tell me something about El Chile. How close would it be to the city of San Vicente? I know they grow coffee, but I think there are oranges, too. But it's mostly coffee, I think—isn't that true?"

"Yes, of course," he smiled reassuringly. "Yes, in that area much coffee is grown." I couldn't decide whether he sensed something beyond my words, or was merely humoring me. "One moment, please," he said, holding up his index finger to keep my attention while he turned to a student who asked him about labor union organizing in the urban areas. Another wanted to know more about the notorious right-wing death squads. Another student wondered if he could see for himself the torture scars which the FMLN representative said he still had—and was he not afraid to speak publicly after all he had been through? What about his family, after all?

The FMLN representative replied that he had stopped being afraid long ago, and that he had little fear for his relatives since most of his family members and friends were already dead. Within ten minutes the FMLN representative had given brief, polite answers to all the questions, no matter how naive. Now he gathered his papers from the lectern and turned to go.

"Please," I said, catching the sleeve of his jacket. "I only want some verification. In your lecture you mentioned the area around the San Vicente volcano, and I think that even though it is very small, El Chile must be important. With all the fighting there, it must be important."

"Oh," he stopped and faced me. "How do you mean?"

"I know it," I said. "I know of people from there and around there who were killed. I have a daughter who tells me. I adopted her six months ago, and she remembers everything. Her sister went to live in El Chile, and as far as I know she could still be there. It is terrible to know a place intimately, yet not be able to find it on a map."

The FMLN representative kept his eyes fixed on mine, and I continued, "It is not that I don't believe the stories my daughter tells me, but I have never talked to an adult about El Chile. I don't even know how it is spelled. My daughter doesn't either, you understand, because nobody in her family could read. All I want is some kind of adult verification. Is it really El Chile? Is it spelled like the country? It all seems so horrible, so incredible." I felt the tears come to my eyes. "Tell me, is it all true?"

The FMLN representative sighed. "This has been an embattled area, and we held it on and off for several years. There have been many killings and raids—what the government calls clean-up operations. More recently, the army has been forcibly evacuating the peasant population from the entire volcano."

"Oh," I exclaimed, feeling completely at a loss now that he had answered my question. "Where do you think the people from El Chile could be?"

The FMLN representative laughed out loud, but I wasn't embarrassed; he was obviously laughing at the absurdity of a situation much larger than mine. After all, there were thousands of places like El Chile in El Salvador. His face became grave once again. Behind a wall of sorrow and detachment, and with just a hint of contempt for my privileged concern for only a few individuals, he said matter-of-factly, "Some of the people must have been killed, some fled into the mountains, some were relocated by the army, some wound up in refugee camps, and some probably left the country."

"And if they were young?" I insisted, "a young woman, for example, or an orphaned boy?"

The FMLN representative paused for a moment as he put on his overcoat, sighed for the last time, and headed for the door. "In such a case their chances could be better," he said without looking back at me—"or possibly worse."

The students and the rest of the audience had already left the room. Caught in the web of my ignorance, my determination, and my guilt, I watched the FMLN representative walk through the door and felt utterly foolish and alone.

I found someone who knows about El Chile," I said to María who was still awake in bed when I came home. "He says there was a lot of fighting there."

"Of course," she said, "I tell you lots of time. Don't you remember?"

"But I didn't realize it was a liberated zone for a time."

"What it mean?"

"It means a place for—libertad."

"Oh," she yawned. "Chile was high up and beautiful. We like to work there much better than for the fat man in San Antonio who doesn't pay much and doesn't let my father have time for the dinner. We like to sleep under the coffee trees when we are sweating and hot from the work, and nobody get mad at us. In Chile are many, many oranges, and we pick so many oranges we want to eat. That's why we like it so much, and—"

"But there was fighting," I interrupted.

"Yes, Mamá, there was the fighting. I tell you already. The soldados from down there in their big house like the castle came up and try to kill the other soldados way up there."

"Did you really see both kinds of soldiers? Were you actually there during the fighting? Or did you hear about it?"

"We try not to be there when was the fighting. Mamá,

you have to understand, nobody likes to be there in the fighting. But sometimes we had to go to Chile because we need the work and the money. Anyhow we liked to be with Marta, because we missed her so much and little Marinita. But many of the times were the soldados from down there and the bombas and the planes. Sometimes the soldados standed in the street a long time watching us."

"And where was Marta? And Miguel?"

"After my father died, Miguel cry a long time and want to go with a gun out. But my mother say he was too young and had to stay with us in the coffee. He was mad at my mother and didn't like it."

"And where were the men and the women?"

"Well?" María shrugged, yawned, and closed her eyes. "What else? They had to go out and protect."

"That was in the mountains?"

"Of course!" María perked up. "Mamá, what a silly question! We were high up—where else should we go? Mamá, please try to understand! When the army soldados come there to chase us and kill us with the bombas and guns, then the mens and the womens have to protect."

"All the women? Even Marta?"

"Some of the womens go out with the mens to protect. The other womens picked the coffee and cooked the food."

"You mean the women who didn't go out to protect."

"Yes, and the older children."

"Like Miguel."

"Yes."

"And the young women like Marta went out to protect."

"No."

"Marta didn't go out to protect sometimes?"

"No."

"Why not?"

"Mamá, you don't understand anything! Marta had three big bellies. You remember? She had little Marinita who cry all the time for her milk. Mamá, please understand! How could Marta just like that go out to protect?"

"Well, what did she do?"

"Mamá, she picked the coffee, I tell you already. And she cooked the food for the others. And she had the belly and she took care of little Marinita."

"And where do you think Marta is now?"

"I think maybe she didn't go down. She told me she would stay up there. She said she saw too many bad things in her life. Too many people were died. Even after her husband died, she said she wanted to stay up there with her friends."

"Where do you think Marta would go if something happened in El Chile?"

María yawned. "Where you think she would go, Mamá?" She yawned again. "You tell me this time. Why you always ask me the question? What you think now? Where she would go?"

"I'm not sure," I said, feeling extremely awkward. "Maybe she would have to go down to San Vicente, or maybe she would go elsewhere on the volcano."

"Yes, Mamá, I think you are right . . . oh, I'm falling asleep." María yawned, and yawned again. "But maybe you're right, Mamá. Maybe someday you understand. Maybe that's where Marta would go . . . somewhere down there, or farther up."

It was an unusually hot Saturday afternoon. The leaves were maroon, green, and gold—the colors of Indian summer. I was reading a book on the back deck when María walked past me carrying the clothes hamper. After setting it down on the grass, she hurried back into the house and brought from the basement the styrofoam kickboard we had used at the pool during the summer. She ran back once more and fetched a bar of laundry soap and a scrub brush from under the kitchen sink. The she stripped down to her underpants, picked up the soap, put the first item from the hamper on the styrofoam kickboard she was using as a washboard —and turned on the hose. An hour later, an assortment of women's and girls' T-shirts, socks, underwear, pants, blouses, and skirts lay spread on the grass, drying gloriously in the sun.

"See how is the washing?" María said as she sat down beside me, exhilarated from the success of her work, her skin glowing with water and sweat. "I like it much more better this way than with the machine. The clothes smell more pretty"—and she handed me a light blouse which had already dried.

"Mmmm," I smelled it. "Oh, yes!"

"Mamá," she began, settling back in her chair, her legs dangling playfully, her eyes occasionally checking her responsibilities on the lawn. "After my mother died, we like to pretend with my girl cousins that we were mothers. We took the little ones with us behind our house way up where was a small river. It was not deep, you know, mostly just stones. I remember I like it so much because I washed the clothes for Miguel and my little brothers, and I felt better because I remembered my mother. We older girls washed the clothes, and the little ones played in the water. All around me I looked, and I felt there was my mother. Then, after we were finished, we brought the clothes back and put them on the ground near our house to dry and shine in the sun.

"One of the times we were washing, and one of my cousins—I think it was Gladi—found a dead man near the bushes. His face was down to the ground, and we saw there was blood under him. We were scared, and we all of us took our washing and hurried back to our house to tell the people down there. Pretty soon some of the mens from the houses over there came up and carried the man down. I didn't like to find there the dead man, but many of the times I was just happy when I was washing the clothes for Miguel and my little brothers. Because I washed and looked around and felt— there was my mother."

María came over and sat on my lap. After a while, she began again, "There is a saying, 'On the day you die, you are happy.' Maybe it's not true, but that's what my mother tell me one day. Anyway, I know, on the day she died she was happy. She put on her orange dress, and she was going with us in the night to the feria. But Miguel was mad. He say it was too dangerous, she shouldn't go there. But my mother say that day she didn't care anymore, she want to be happy. Anyway, one of the mens who live near us came to there with us to protect.

I think he like my mother and want to marry her. But she tell him she only loved my father and didn't want anybody else. Anyway, I remember he come with us some of the times and protect us and carry things for my mother. So that night we left the little ones at home with Miguel and my grandparents, and I went to the feria with my girl cousins and my tías and my mother and the man.

"When we were waiting for the rueda I sat next to my mother. She was a little sad. She said she had a feeling something was going to happen to her. She want very much to go on the rueda, but inside she was sad. I think maybe death was inside her already.

"I went with my cousins to go to the bathroom, and my tía Pilar go with us. Maybe we were gone a little time, and my mother and the man and my tía Olivia go up on the rueda. When we were coming back with my cousins, there was much noise and I saw the people. Then I saw my mother. She was lying on the ground. She was sighing, it hurt her so much. Oh, oh, she was making the sounds, so soft, you could almost not hear her. There was a big spot right up here close to her shoulder. It was too much blood, it hurt her so much. I hold her hand a little bit. She didn't say anything, only the soft sounds, but with her eyes I know she was talking to me. Then the Cruz Verde take her to the hospital. I walk with my tía Pilar and we follow her there.

"We waited outside on the bench with my tía Pilar. I already felt inside my mother would die, but Pilar cry and tell me there is hope. My mother died in the night. The nurse tell us she was sorry, it was too late. My mother was inside all blood, and her back was broken because she fell to the hard ground from the rueda. Then we went home, and they brought our mother the next day in the box to our house.

"They put our mother in the house next door that was

empty because of the bones—the one they call the house of the dead. It's where they have the party for her. I tell you already Miguel was so mad, and when we tell him about our mother he shot a gun at the sky. And I tell you Marta faint three times when she saw my mother in the box. They have to put the little bottle under her nose the three times. Then I remember I watch her put on our mother's black dress.

"The next day we had the big party for my mother, and we stayed a long time next to the box. Many peoples came from the houses to see our mother, they like her so much. The man who want to marry her came with his leg broken, and he was jumping. He and my tía Olivia didn't fall all the way down from the rueda. It was only my mother who fall.

"But my mother's eyes didn't close, she didn't want to leave us. Aurelio and I tried to close her eyes, but she kept them open a long time. The white sheet was around her in the box, and we put in the orange dress and the green dress with the little white buttons and the collar—if the spirit came back, just in case. But when her spirit came to me later she was standing in a long beautiful white dress—she looked so pretty. Anyway, her dresses went with her, just in case.

"Then we watched her and we waited, and we put our hands on her eyes one more time. Then she closed them. She must have thought it was time, her spirit was ready. The first day she kept her eyes open, but the next day she let us close them. Then some of the people went to dig a hole, I don't know where. I stayed at home with my little brothers, and the others went out and they buried our mother somewhere."

31

"**What's this? Where** you get it?" María's voice was unusually shrill as she picked up a card from the pile of mail on the hall table. It was a postcard showing the signature of the Salvadoran death squads, *mano blanca,* the mark of a white hand placed on the doors of slain political activists and peasant organizers. The university gallery was advertising an exhibition of photographs from El Salvador, and the postcard was clearly intended to unsettle.

"It's just an advertisement. It came in the mail," I said with an air of indifference. "A lot of them were probably sent to people to tell them that they can go to a building at the university and look at pictures of the war in El Salvador. It's nothing more, just a card."

"But where it come from? Why it come here, to us?"

"Don't worry," I said, putting my arms around María's rigid body. "It's not real, they're just pictures. I know it must sound strange to you, but this is one way that people in the United States can find out what is happening in El Salvador. If they know what is happening, maybe they can help. Believe me, this exhibition is a good thing, and the people who are organizing it want to help. The card that came in the mail is only telling us about the pictures so that people can see them. It's not the real thing."

María seemed more disturbed than incredulous. Her body had assumed the familiar withholding gesture of fear. "María, do you know this picture?" I asked, stroking her head with one hand and holding the card with the mano blanca in the other. "Have you ever seen it?"

"No!" she blanched and turned away.

"It's the mano blanca. You know what that is, don't you?"

"No!"

"It's the sign they leave after they kill the people. I have a feeling you know it."

"Why should I know it?"

"Well, maybe you've heard of it, or seen it."

"I don't know."

"They don't wear uniforms like the army or the Guardias or the police. They dress in regular clothes and sometimes they wear bandannas over their eyes. They pretend to be guerrilleros so that the government can blame the guerrilleros. They have killed many campesinos like that. You know that, don't you?"

"No!"

"María, you told me that men with masks and knives were looking for your father and other members of your family up in the mountains. You told me that they killed somebody who wanted to stay and sleep in his own house. I think those men with masks and knives must have been like the mano blanca. Don't you think so?"

"I don't think anything," María said firmly, glaring at me.

"All right, we don't have to talk about it any more," I said. "But this card says that next week they are showing pictures of the war in El Salvador, and I'm going to see them. Sometimes pictures can show the truth to people who can't see how things are by themselves. Looking at those pictures is going to be like listening to your stories. You don't need to look at the pictures because you were there and you've seen enough. But I'm going to see them so that I can learn more things and try to understand."

María had long since retreated into her own world and was staring impassively at the floor. I felt overwhelmed by the irony of the situation, frustrated by my own helplessness. Most of all I felt angry at the world for causing María so much pain. Why did it have to continue? As usual, I tried to solve the problem by dragging out the drawing paper and coloring books.

"You and I are going to sit down together right here and color for a while," I said in a determined voice as I took María's arm. She reluctantly followed me. "Maybe you can let go of some of your fear, and I'll vent my anger at everybody who has ever made you scared. But first I'm going to rip up this postcard and throw it in the wastebasket—because it's a weird idea by a bunch of gringos who wanted to get our attention. Really, it's just a piece of paper with a sign on it that doesn't mean a thing to us at this moment. Because I tell you, the reality of it is over for you."

As I ripped the card in half and walked toward the wastebasket, María looked up quickly and smiled at me.

A week later, I went with a couple of my colleagues from the university to the exhibition showing photographs from El Salvador by thirty international photographers. As we stood in front of the photographs we talked about the war, the inability of the Salvadoran government to control the military, and the Reagan administration's continued acceleration of military aid. We talked knowledgeably about the latest findings of Amnesty International, citing statistics of human rights violations with detached looks of concern. At one point, one of my colleagues asked about María. I said she was fine and learning to read at her new school. Some bridges I was no longer able to cross.

I bought an exhibition catalogue and brought it home. Late at night, long after María had gone to sleep, I looked at the pictures again, at every detail in the hundred black-and-white photographs showing life and death in El Salvador since 1979—two-thirds of María's lifetime. At 1 A.M. my head was throbbing, my eyes were peeled open in horror. Oh yes, oh yes, the truth was visible to the large naked eye.

That night I made my decision. María and I had to cross this abyss of memory and come out alive on the other side. I wanted to know the truth, and I had to be ruthless. I put my parenting and psychology books aside, because they didn't help any longer. In their place went the exhibition catalogue.

32

The following Satur- day afternoon I brought the book of photographs to María. I didn't care any more about comparing her truth with that of another. I was no longer interested in my emotional denial, my gnawing disbelief. I only needed her help to figure out how to find the truth and live with the truth—for me, as well as for her.

"María," I said after we had sat down and I had put the exhibition catalogue on the coffee table. "You see this photograph? Are these soldiers?"

"No, it's the Guardias. They always wear the uniforms like that. You see all the silver buttons?—they're so shiny."

"What are they doing?"

"They are taking the people away in a truck."

"The people are lying on top of each other. They look as if they are dead."

"No, they have to be lying like that. They've been ordered. If they are dead they are turned around maybe, with their faces looking at the sky. Now the Guardias are just taking them somewhere."

"Where are they taking the people?"

"To the place where they hit them and kill them."

"Where is that place?"

"I don't know. I think anywhere."

"What are they doing in this picture over here? Is it the Guardias?"

"No, it's the army soldiers."

"It looks as if they're tying the people up."

"No. They are looking for the names on the cards. See, it's like this. First they make the people lie on the ground and looking down. They have to be like this, in a line. Their hands have to be behind their heads. See, that's how they have them. You see all of them? Like this? The army soldados check their names to see if they are looking for them. If they find one they're looking for, they shoot. Or maybe just all of them, they shoot. Or almost all. But sometimes they don't shoot. Sometimes just everybody has to be in a line, and nobody shoots."

"María, did you ever have to be in a line?"

"Yes! Of course! How else can I know?"

"Was it in San Antonio?"

No answer.

"Was it near the house in the woods where you lived with your parents after San Antonio?"

No answer.

"Was it in San Vicente?"

No answer.

"Well, how was it for the other people when they were in a line?"

"The army came to the place and the people have to line up standing. Once they standed a long time. The army soldiers were looking for somebody. That's what they said. Then they called out some people. They called them out with their fingers, like this. They pointed. This one, and that one, and the next one, children, too. And the one over there, and the next one. The others stood there a long time and watched in the line.

"And what happened?"

"The ones they called out and killed."

"And what did the other people do?"

"They cried and tried to help, but some people held them back and said, no, then everybody is killed."

"And what happened then?"

"After they finished killing the people, the soldados went away with their trucks."

"And then?"

"Nothing. The people made the graves and buried them."

"And the children?"

"The ones they were left?"

"Yes."

"They helped burying them."

"And what did the people do then? Did they leave that place because it wasn't safe anymore?"

"No. They went back to their houses."

"What did they do in their houses?"

"They went all to the one bed and cried. They put their arms holding each other and try to sleep."

"Did they leave that place the next day because it wasn't safe?"

"No. They had to earn the money. The next day they had to go up there early to work in the fields."

"And the children? It must have been very bad for the children."

No answer. We sat in silence. Slowly I turned the pages of the book.

"Oh, look at this one," María said after a few minutes. "You see this picture? Remember I tell you the bombas and the guns from the sky? The big one up there, you see it? That's one of them, I remember. That's like the ones they shoot from the sky."

"Yes," I said. "They call it a Huey helicopter." I flipped

some more pages until I came to a picture of a dance in a guerrilla camp. The men and women were dancing close together, their rifles slung over their shoulders. "What are these people doing?" I asked. "Who are they?"

"Soldados, the ones in the mountains. They are dancing and holding each other because they are afraid tomorrow they die. They look like the soldados who try to protect us. But sometimes when they are coming it is not good for us, because the army soldados come from the other direction and want to kill us. So when the soldados come from the mountains we cry, 'Watch out, here come the soldados,' because we know there will be fighting and we are in the middle. You see the picture, they don't have the real uniforms. Some of them don't have any at all. They are poor, like us. You see, some of the uniforms are messy and funny. You see, the soldados?"

"Yes, I see." I turned a few more pages, trying to pass over the photographs of murdered peasants in the countryside. But María had become engrossed and began leafing again toward the front of the book. One photograph in particular interested her.

"Oh, here, look! Mamá, you see the white in this picture? You see it around the man in the box, all the way to the head? You see it?"

"Yes. What about it?"

"It's what they put around my mother. It looked exactly like that! You see? Remember I tell you, the white? You see? It's not really a dress. It's white like a blanket, see?"

"Yes, I see."

"It looked just like that. See how clear is the little window? See how close you can see his face through the window? His eyes are closed, and it looks like sleeping. Oh no, the face is not the same, but the white. My mother looked just like that in the box. First her eyes stayed open. We tried, but she didn't let us close them. But then, after we stayed next to the box and watched a long time, then she let us close her eyes. She looked just peaceful and asleep. Like this, you see?"

"Yes, I see. Look, there are some words written on the glass. They must have been written by the man's wife."

"What they say?"

"I can't make out the writing in Spanish, but down here under the picture there is a translation. It says: 'I love you, I will never forget you, I will tell my daughter about you when she grows up and can understand.' It says he was killed in a demonstration in front of the Rosario Church in San Salvador. Twenty-four of them were killed."

"Poor little girl," María sighed, "Maybe his daughter was very little. Maybe she was too little to understand."

PART

3

Underground Railroad,
Southward

They called it San Antonio and probably they still do. *Who knows what is there now and who is? Some people tried to go back to live, but it was no more. The houses were burned, and the bodies. Everything was burned after they killed the people—it dropped from the planes like fire from the sky. So the green from the trees was swept gray-black into the wind above the volcano. They called this one hamlet San Antonio, and it was a young bald head scraped hard with a razor. Nothing was left and nothing was future. Nothing was left but the stories and the mind's pictures of dust and wind.*

No, it was not a dream, never a dream. The dreams tell the future, and the stories tell the past. The rest is the middle. Cándida, you were in the middle. When you dream something it will come true, you had told María de Jesús. But the stories held the words of the past, and the dreams were nothing any longer. You had heard the stories, you knew the dreams; and you were in the middle. You took your hands from your eyes and your ears, and you raised your fists into the silence of nothing. Then your sorrow was boundless, and you opened your mouth of whispers to speak what you knew.

María de Jesús was the world, and the sun was her mother. But she knew the sun had gone dark, it dropped out of the sky. The day was up in the morning, it went down at night. Still she was spinning around with the time. It was the same speed and the same time, always the rhythm, but the center was empty and nothing. Each day she heard your voice, knew your face and your spidery brown fingers. Each night she saw your orange dress spilled, and remembered your sigh and the

169

feeling. Her stomach was empty, but her mouth wanted nothing. She had hung from your nape and sat tight on your hip. From you she knew every leaf, every fruit. You had shown her how to pick it and open it, to peel it and taste it, to eat or not eat the pit. She remembered the chop, chop, snap, snap, the scrubbing and wiping, the flap, flap of making tortillas. She remembered how before the words and between the words everything had its shape, form, place. She remembered the short, cupped sleeve of your green dress, knew the voice and the stories. She was spinning around each day and each night, but it was dark all the day and empty at night. The sun had gone dark and dropped out of the sky, and she knew the thin line of space between something and nothing.

Cándida, high up in the dark sky the stars made you a crystalline bed. It was there your father-in-law José pointed out you and Felipe to your orphaned children. They were sitting with their cousins around the fire, looking up, listening to their grandfather's stories about your ancestors and the animals outlined by the lights in the sky. It was the fire outside the hut next to the house of the dead on the outskirts of San Vicente. All had become silent now, except for the lingering gunshots.

It was early 1983. Salvadoran newspapers reported another massive mobilization by the armed forces with the objective of eliminating all suspected subversives from the San Vicente volcano. Citizens of the city of San Vicente reported waking to hear explosions on the slopes of the volcano, seeing Air Force Fouga planes dive to drop the bombs that rocked the earth. Three helicopters flying east of San Vicente were directing the planes' operations. In April, during fighting between government and FMLN forces in the town of Verapaz on one of the slopes of Chinchontepec, the townspeople saw guerrillas pick up the body of a commander and carry it by mule toward the volcano.

That spring, your eldest daughter Marta and her child may have escaped death farther up on the volcano. On the outskirts of San Vicente, the surviving members of Felipe's family went on living from hand to mouth among the rubble and decay. On one of those spring mornings, your eldest son Miguel and your three youngest children started out on the road to the state orphanage in Ilopango.

Over the Christmas hol- idays we traveled to Washington, D.C. I had made contact there with a Salvadoran social scientist who had been an adviser to the land reform program in the early 1980s. After receiving repeated death threats from right-wing death squads, he became a political exile in the United States, where he presented lectures and testified before congressional committees. María and I had come on the appointed day to his small apartment in the Adams-Morgan district. Before long we found ourselves watching the large, robust man spread out a map that covered an entire dining room table.

"Well, well, let us look and see," he said in his jolly voice while his fingers carefully followed tiny veinlike roads to the south of the city of San Vicente. "This is a pretty good map of the province of San Vicente," he mused. "If your San Antonio is to the southeast of the provincial capital, it is bad, very bad. But come, first let us look and see."

We stepped closer to the table. The province was shaped like the continent of South America. We were looking at the equivalent of somewhere in the northeastern corner of Bolivia. Although the province of San Vicente looked gigantic on the table, the actual size of our search was in miniature.

"These are all small winding dirt roads," said Julio. "The trucks that pick up the people once a week to bring them to the market in the capital have a tough time." I could hear María's breathing as we followed the circular movements of his fingers with our eyes. "Well, well," he chuckled, and we probed the fine lines, letters, and dots. "You see, so far I have found three San Antonios just to the south of the provincial capital. I told you, there could be a hundred San Antonios in the entire country," he said with a laugh and a slow, incredulous shake of his head.

"Dime, María. Tell me." Julio put his big arm around her as they looked together at the map. No, she shook her head, it took long, but not so very long to go to San Vicente. No, they hardly ever walked from San Antonio. No, they didn't have to stop and change—the truck went straight to San Vicente. Yes, they went this way when the truck reached the big road. The other way was with the truck to the other market when they went to her sister in El Chile. Yes, she thought she remembered railroad tracks. Yes, she clearly remembered the sound of the train on their way toward San Vicente.

"There was a train nearby us after we had to leave San Antonio," María told me the next day. "I remember because once we heard there were cows on the track, and the driver was yelling at them to move away. Everybody was yelling, but you know the train cannot stop so fast. The cows didn't know they should move, so they were run over and some of them died. Even though the cows were dead, we were happy because Miguel ran with some people to get food. He was still a boy and not so strong, so he only brought one leg from a cow. Still, it was big, and we ate it a long time."

"Well, well, we have probably found the place," said Julio about ten minutes later, his arm still around María. "Come, see for yourself." He motioned to me. "You see, it must be this one over here to the southeast, as I feared." He put a plump finger under a mesh of lines and rows of dots—"The one, you can see, fairly close to the railroad tracks. It was very bad in that area a few years ago, very bloody." He stopped. I could see that he had tears in his eyes. "Most people didn't survive in that part of the province," he said, looking down at María. "She was lucky."

María stared at the huge map on the table. Her long, thin index finger covered many of the tiny roads that ran from the surrounding hamlets toward the provincial capital, but the nail of her finger had scratched the hint of an incision into the paper of the map. Just beyond that incision was printed in fine but unmistakable letters the name "San Antonio Caminos." San Antonio of the Roads. The hamlet was situated on two dirt roads joined like a horseshoe and leading two-pronged down to the main highway between the cities San Vicente and Zacatecoluca, the capital of the next province.

Suddenly María seemed very stiff. "Ah, mira! Our friends have come to visit!" Julio exclaimed. Six people, laughing and joking in Spanish, filed into the room and sat down.

"Oh yes, how good to meet you, the guests from out of town. We have heard about you, María and her mother. Hello, hello. How are you?"

"Hello, we are so glad to meet you," I said, turning to nod toward María. But she was still standing straight and tense next to the table. Her hand was still on the map, her index finger right under the dot and the incision marking her San Antonio.

"It is very hard to be here, I know, very hard," said one of the women after a while. She came over and spoke to María in a mixture of Spanish and English. "It is so very hard." She turned her head back and gestured toward the others in the room. "You see, everyone in this room had to leave El Salvador sometime in the last five years. Every one of us left parents and sisters and brothers behind. And you know, each of us has somebody in our family who was killed. You know about that, don't you, how the people are killed?"

María nodded her head without a word. She looked straight at the floor. The tears began to roll down her face, and she concentrated all her energy on preventing herself from surrendering to her tears. "Everyone in this room has loved somebody who was killed," continued the woman. "You must not forget it. You must look at us. You know how it was, but you are not the only one. Yes, I know it is terrible." The woman held María's shaking body. "I know how terrible it was. Every one of us in this room knows it, and we live with it every day. You are not alone. There are many of us who know it. We are all living with it, never forget that. You are not alone with it, little one. You are not alone."

This was the map. This upside-down pear shape was the province of San Vicente. In the middle of the province was the provincial capital, just a few kilometers south of the east-west Pan American Highway. Connecting the city of San Vicente with the Pan American Highway was the north-south highway. By all indications a two-lane paved road, it led directly south to a town called Tecoluca, then southwest to Zacatecoluca, the capital of the province of La Paz. This was the very road—I traced the line with my index finger—taken by the trucks carrying María's family five kilometers north to the market in San Vicente on Saturday mornings, the same road taken in the opposite direction, about fifteen kilometers southwest, by the trucks carrying them to the market in Zacatecoluca. There they must have changed to the other truck that went in a northerly direction on a small winding dirt road, about seven kilometers straight up the volcano to El Chile—now I had found it!—on the western side of Chinchontepec, in the remote northeast corner of the province of La Paz. With the transfer in Zacatecoluca and all the possible stops at hamlets along the way—La Ceiba, San Diego, El Cumbo, El Arco, and so forth—as well as the town of Tecoluca, the trip to El Chile could have taken several hours.

In the end, María had told me, the north-south highway was no longer passable because of continuous army massacres at hamlets along the route. The two-lane paved highway, which she called the big road, was itself unsafe. Trucks filled with campesinos were stopped, the passengers searched, many of them killed. I recognized the names of some of the hamlets where there had been large-scale army massacres: El Campanario, San Benito, La Pita, El Puente, La Lucha—all of them between ten and fifteen kilometers from San Antonio, just off the north-south highway, right on the border between the provinces of San Vicente and La Paz.

On their earlier rides to El Chile, María and her brothers must have stood in the backs of trucks with children from these hamlets, their faces held high into the wind, their hair slicked back, their mouths wide in delight at the speed. Then the trucks could no longer pass, and the children were bones scattered on the dirt and the grass. Then María and her mother and her brothers went farther north and took the long way around the northern slopes of the volcano to visit Marta and work in the coffee fields. At that time the towns of Guadalupe and Veracruz on the northern slopes of Chinchontepec were held by the FMLN.

I knew that fighting in the province of San Vicente had intensified in 1982. The government forces held the capital and most of the areas south of it, but the FMLN, with strong popular support around the provincial capital and on the slopes of the volcano, had made inroads from the north. But the province of San Vicente was not Chalatenango, nor Morazan, nor San Miguel, where the terrain was rough and the opposition could hold out for years in the hills. Practically the entire province of San Vicente was cultivated, with one finca and one hacienda after the other. It was one of the most prosperous agricultural regions in El Salvador, and the government forces were everywhere. Photographs in books published before the war showed idyllic pastoral scenes—rich green fields along dirt roads where men, women, and children walked to and from work in the morning and evening sun. San Vicente was hardly an ideal place for strategic opposition. Everyone was an open target.

In the space of that one year, 1982, half María's family members were killed—her father, her grandmother, three uncles, an aunt, her godparents, her brother-in-law. The home she had known was razed to the ground, and villagers who returned to San Antonio after the army had left said that everything had been burned and only weeds sprouted where formerly crops had grown and houses stood. Late in that year María's mother died from a fall in a barrio on the outskirts of the city of San Vicente. The battles on the streets and on the volcano continued long after she died, and her youngest children went into the streets searching for food. After a few months they were taken to the state orphanage by their oldest brother. The gringos arrived a year later, and the three youngest were adopted.

It was late, and I was tired from the long day. I rolled up the map and went upstairs. María and I were staying with old friends of mine who lived in Washington. As I passed María's room—a cot had been made up for her in the study—I noticed that the light was still on. She was in bed, staring at something in a large book.

I sat down next to her on the cot and saw that she was looking at color plates of paintings by Pieter Brueghel the Elder. As soon as I had sat down, she quickly flipped back the pages till she stopped to show me *The Wedding Dance*.

"See, Mamá, see how the people are dancing outside, next to the trees."

"Yes," I said, pleased that of all the books she might have

picked up in this study she had found Brueghel, the sixteenth-century Flemish painter whose rendering of peasant life would surely have affirmed her own.

"It was like that in Salvador. We were just all of us together, and we had the big parties."

"Yes," I said, settling back more comfortably against the pillow, amazed, as always, by Brueghel's extraordinary realism and color.

"And Mamá, look here"—María turned to another page.

It was *The Harvesters.* We gazed in silence at the harvesting of grain on top of a hill overlooking an immense plain. A few men in white shirts and broad hats worked with their scythes, while in the distance three women carried sheaves of grain over their shoulders down the slope of the hill leading to the plain. In the background, next to the shocks of grain, a few figures, men and women, were bent over, tying up stalks. In the foreground peasants were eating together under a lone tree that shaded them from the sun. One of the women turned back to cut more bread from the loaf in her basket, while a man lay sprawled supine next to his scythe on the other side of the tree trunk. A boy in short trousers drank milk from a bowl at the far right edge of the group.

"Is this how it was when you were up in the sugarcane?" I asked María.

"I think yes," she murmured, her thoughts clearly back in another time. She was quiet for a few moments, then said, "But Mamá, look"—and swiftly turned to another page.

It was *The Massacre of the Innocents,* a portrayal of Herod's proclamation against first-born sons. But, as always with Brueghel, the soldiers and peasants were in sixteenth-century dress, making the contemporary political allusion unmistakable. The text accompanying the plate mentioned that the troops of the Duke of Alba had been asserting the supremacy of the Spanish empire against rebellious villages and peasant factions.

On the right-hand side of the painting a cavalry soldier sat on his horse commanding mercenaries in peasant dress as they attacked a house. In back of them villages surrounded a wealthy man astride a horse, pleading with him to intervene. In the center background a group of uniformed soldiers hacked a child to death while women cried in despair, clinging to their children. With their lances held high, a column of fully armored soldiers on horseback watched the scene. In the foreground, a peasant family—the man kneeling before the horse, his cap beside him on the ground—begged one of the officers to spare their child.

"Look at the soldados," said María.

"Yes." I told her about the Bible story.

"Did they have the soldados when Jesús live?" she asked.

"Yes," I said.

She swallowed carefully and was quiet for a few moments. Then she suggested: "But the people don't dress like this. They have more long clothes, and even the men have the long dresses and long hair. I know, because once my mother take me to the big church in San Vicente and I see the statues. They were so pretty. But they don't wear the pants and the hats like the people here."

"That's because the picture here is not only about Jesus' time. It's about the time when the painter lived, and so the people are dressed in the clothes they wore at that time. It was a long time ago—four hundred years ago."

"Did they have the Guardias then, too—and the soldados?"

"Yes," I said.

"Like Salvador? And they killed the people?"

"Yes." It was already after midnight, and I wanted to stay

with the memory of Brueghel's happy depictions of peasant life—the greeting-card kind. "Let's close the book now and get some sleep," I said.

"Mamá, just look at the one more picture"—she flipped pages and found what she was looking for.

It was *The Triumph of Death*, an immense barren landscape with armies, gallows, and smoking fires in the background. In the foreground were dying and decomposing bodies, cartloads of skulls, and armies of skeletons marching in from all sides.

"See Mamá, I always try to tell you," said María after a while. "This the way it look after the people die and we were so lonely and scared. See how it is just the bones and the dead bodies everywhere? See, now you can see."

"Yes, I see," I said to María, closing the book, putting my arms around her, telling her that I would stay beside her while she slept. "Yes, now I can see," I repeated as she closed her eyes and pushed her head close to me. "Now I can see."

Sitting on the bed, waiting for María to fall asleep, I let my head droop. My mind wandered from the book on my lap and the map of San Vicente rolled up on the night table beside me. After a series of low dark skies and dreary winter-blue landscapes, I dreamed of myself as a child on a farm in Europe at the end of the Second World War. It was April 1945. The cold morning air was thick with mist. I was in the farmyard at dawn, waiting for the farmer and his wife to finish their chores and come out of the warm, steamy stable. It was connected by a small door to the large whitewashed farmhouse with green shutters where I lived upstairs. The S.S. and other German army units which had occupied the farmyard for several days on their retreat were gone. Today we would continue the planting. The scene shifted. Dressed in layers of scratchy wool sweaters, stockings, undergarments, a field-gray skirt made from an old army blanket, and with a light blue headscarf pulled down over my forehead, I sat expectantly between the farmer and his wife at the front of the heavy wagon. Muttering encouragement to the two nags, Farmer Renner adjusted the reins, slapped them in the air a few centimeters above the horses' flanks, and shouted "Wiah, Fani . . . Wiah, Moah. . . ." The wheels creaked, and the horses slowly pulled their load toward the village road, their hooves sinking one by one into the muddy gullies and shallow icy puddles left by yesterday's tank treads. As we turned onto the road, I heard Frau Renner saying the rosary under her breath. A sharp wind came up, and the names of the millions of the dead swept by my ears. When we arrived at the field, I jumped to the loamy ground. It was the earth roaring across the centuries under my feet.

CHAPTER

35

I knew I could not rest vadoran daily news-
until María's stories papers, the right-wing
were framed in the *El Diario de Hoy* and
language of historical the ultra-right-wing
discourse, until I found the *La Prensa Gráfica,* both con-
written connection between taining information and edi-
her world and mine. The next torializing from the per-
day, I drove up the coast and spective of the dominant gov-
took María to stay at my ernment, army, and business
mother's. Then I went back to sectors. Films from the For-
Washington and spent a week eign Broadcast Information
in the newspaper and peri- Service (FBIS), which sum-
odical room of the Library marizes and translates news
of Congress. Scanning hun- from major international
dreds of reels of microfilm wire services for U.S. govern-
for recorded facts pertinent ment agencies, provided into María's life, I tried to plot a formation about El Salvador
line of history that would fill from French, Mexican, and
in the spaces and silences of Cuban wire services; sum-
her world. Who else would maries of the progovernment
make the connection, if not I? *El Mundo, Diario Latino,* and

The Library of Congress *Radio Cadena YSKL* in San Sal-
held microfilms of the two Sal- vador; and FMLN broadcasts

over *Radio Farabundo Martí* and *Radio Venceremos,* often directly from the respective battlefronts. Among major U.S. and European dailies, I looked for news about the area of San Vicente and the volcano Chinchontepec in the *New York Times,* the *Washington Post,* the *Los Angeles Times,* and the *San Francisco Chronicle,* as well as checking sporadically in the *London Times, Manchester Guardian, Neue Züricher Zeitung, Frankfurter Allgemeine,* and *Le Monde.* I began my search with the year 1978. Most news about the area, I quickly learned, focused on 1982.

"Early today some 2,000 soldiers began the first military operation of 1982 around San Vicente Volcano," *Radio Cadena* reported on January 7, 1982. "Military sources told our station that some 2,000 soldiers and members of the Atlacatl battalion as well as jet planes have joined the operation to drive out completely the subversives from the San Vicente Volcano. The sources did not disclose the planned length of the military operation. This is confidential information to protect the operation against subversion."

"The army, waging a three-pronged air and ground assault on guerrilla mountain camps southeast of the capital, claimed yesterday it destroyed a jungle hideout of the leftists," wrote the *San Francisco Chronicle* on January 9, 1982. "The push, launched Thursday on the slopes of a volcanic peak with 1500 troops and 500 civilian paramilitary forces, was yielding 'positive results,' according to a military communiqué. . . . Residents of San Vicente, the area of the government offensive, said there was heavy artillery fire on the slopes of Mount Chinchontepec. They reported the government was using planes and helicopters in the drive, the sixth offensive against guerrilla hideouts on the mountain."

On January 9 the *Los Angeles Times* reported: "An 1800-man force of government troops closed in Friday on a guerrilla stronghold on the slopes of a volcano, but Salvadoran military officials conceded that many of the rebels had already escaped. . . . Most of the casualties, including a lieutenant, were reported south of the volcano, near the town of Tecoluca, where a patrol apparently tripped a guerrilla land mine."

From the map of the province I knew that Tecoluca was six kilometers directly south of San Antonio. By this time María, her parents, and her brothers, as well as her father's family, must already have left. They were living in the woods right outside San Vicente. There she and Miguel found the bones around their house and daily saw Jeeps with army soldiers—"wearing wide round helmets, the top crossed like a pie"—pass by indifferently on roads strewn with corpses. She had already observed how her godparents had been killed.

On January 10, the *Washington Post* printed an AP wire report from Fort Bragg, North Carolina: "Sixty sergeants and officers from El Salvador arrived today to begin 16 weeks of basic infantry training with the Green Berets. . . . In nearby Fayetteville, people opposed to the training gathered to plan a demonstration. . . . The protesters contend troops of Salvadoran President José Napoleon Duarte have killed 30,000 civilians in two years and imprisoned and tortured thousands more. Fort Bragg officials said before the leaders landed that the 36 Salvadoran army sergeants and 24 officers will get one month of training in military leadership before a 1,000-man army battalion arrives from the Central American nation in mid-February. Spokesmen for the pentagon have said another 600 Salvadoran soldiers will go to Fort Benning, Ga., beginning Jan. 25."

"Operation Petronilo, the antiguerrilla drive conducted by the Salvadoran Armed Forces over the weekend in the foothills of Chinchontepec volcano . . . left 20 guerrillas and 2 soldiers dead, and several wounded on both sides," reported the Paris AFP wire service on January 11. "Over 2,000 troops from the armed forces' engineers' training center, the 5th Infantry Brigade headquartered in San Vicente, artillery units and the Atlacatl battalion—the counterinsurgency unit trained by U.S. advisors—participated in operation Petronilo."

On January 23, the *New York Times* reported, "A clandestine radio station said today that two United States military advisers took part in a Salvadoran Army attack this month in which 70 civilians were slain. The assertion was denied by the United States Embassy. Radio Venceremos said the advisers were seen directing an artillery barrage in an army attack Jan. 5–9 of guerrilla strongholds on Chinchontepec volcano, 35 miles east of the capital. The attack was backed by 105 millimeter artillery pieces installed in the Jiboa sugar mill and under the command of two American advisers who were directing the fire on our positions,' it said."

FBIS reported the clandestine *Radio Farabundo Martí's* January 26 "live relay from unidentified war correspondent of the people's liberation forces in the Anastasio Aquino Paracentral Front of the FMLN in San Vicente: 'We denounce the following to the peoples of the world: Today, 25 January, at 1330, the central region of San Vicente Department was once again invaded by members of the armed forces Engineers' Instruction Center in Zacatecoluca. During this operation 50 people, including children and old people, were killed in cold blood. This occurred in (Campanario) canton. The order (?to carry out the murders) was given by officer (name indistinct) of Zacatecoluca. He said the order is to kill everyone who (word indistinct). . . . We call upon the democratic progressive organizations and the International Red Cross to demand an investigation of these crimes which have already cost the lives of more than (?150) people in the past 3 months in this region. Most of those killed have been children and old people."

María's grandmother, her twelve-year-old daughter, and her twin sons must have been killed on one of these days in mid-to-late January. The women and girls were first raped, then put up against a wall next to the local tienda with other villagers. About this I found nothing in the papers. Either the information was totally suppressed, or the residents of the hamlet San Antonio were lost in the numbers, with no one able to inquire after them because the lives of the survivors, too, were endangered.

"President Reagan told Congress yesterday the El Salvador government's human rights record entitles it to receive U.S. aid, and the State Department said it is urgently studying the need to increase assistance to the regime there following an attack by leftist guerrillas Wednesday on the country's main military air base," wrote John M. Goshko in the *New York Times* on January 29. "Reagan's declaration, in the form of a certification to Congress, clears the way for the administration to disburse $26 million in military assistance allotted for El Salvador under the fiscal 1982 foreign aid bill. . . . The president's contention came in a week that saw the American Civil Liberties Union and other human rights groups accuse Salvadoran authorities of continuing repression—including allegedly being responsible for the murder of 12,501 persons during 1981."

On February 1, a reporter for the *Los Angeles Times* wrote, "A top State Department official said today that the Reagan Administration will ask Congress for an increase of about $100 million in assistance to El Salvador this year and will, on its own, send $55 million in emergency military aid to replace aircraft lost in recent guerrilla attacks. . . . Congress in December approved a foreign-aid bill that included $40 million in economic aid and $25 million in military aid for El Salvador. . . . [Assistant Secretary of State Thomas] Enders said the Administration has been unable to confirm press reports of massacres of civilians by Salvadoran security forces in recent weeks. He insisted that there has been 'substantial progress' in the protection of human rights and in other areas."

On February 6, the *Los Angeles Times* printed a report by Dial Torgerson from San Salvador: "An airlift of U.S. helicopters and planes to replace those lost in a rebel attack on a Salvadoran air base began here Friday under secrecy and heavy security. . . . One U.S. official said, 'We don't want anything to happen to any of our Air Force planes.' One C-131 Hercules transport flew into Ilopango on Friday from a Texas air force base, unloaded a 15-seat UH-1H (Huey) helicopter, and left as quickly as possible. The U.S. Embassy here refused to say when other aircraft are due to arrive. Five more Hueys are expected to be delivered. And, according to Washington reports that could not immediately be confirmed here, the United States will also send El Salvador C-123 troop transports, O-2 spotter aircraft and A-37 attack aircraft."

On February 19, *Radio Venceremos* announced, "From 0600 to 1300, FMLN troops clashed with troops of the 5th Infantry Brigade on the Pan-American Highway. At the end of the fighting, the enemy troops were forced to leave the positions which they had held at the San Felipe and Los Cocos turnoffs for 1 week. . . . At 1110, two helicopters and two A-37 planes began indiscriminately bombing our positions and the nearby civilian population. Mr. Reagan recently delivered these planes and helicopters to the fascist junta. Despite the intense bombing and strafing, we remained in position until 1300. We want to report that these new aircraft are being flown by U.S. pilots because the junta doesn't have personnel trained for them yet. . . . We also want to take this opportunity to tell the Salvadoran people and the peoples of the world that (words indistinct) most reactionary sectors of the Honduran Army, who are being trained by green berets, are preparing a new massacre and a new extermination of the civilian population living in our controlled areas in Cabanas and San Vicente Departments."

On February 26, *El Mundo* reported that "units of the Army 5th Infantry Brigade, headquartered in San Vicente, and the security corps were engaged since 0600 today in a fierce clash with a large group of extremists who had launched an attack on San Vicente." *El Mundo* also reported an "extremist attack against San Antonio Caminos." These battles were apparently taking place after the massacre by government troops in January. Nothing more was to be found in any of the sources about San Antonio Caminos, only about El Campanario and other hamlets ten to twelve kilometers farther south.

The *Los Angeles Times* reported on March 7, "Government troops beheaded or shot to death more than 100 peasants in three separate massacres at the end of January around the hamlet of El Campanario, guerrillas said Saturday. A correspondent counted 14 skulls and saw a 10-by-20-foot mass grave outside a church where peasants told him government troops 'lined up people in columns and beheaded them.' Three U.S. correspondents and a U.S. television camera crew were directed to Campanario by contacts in San Salvador. Guerrillas holding the village said the first attack took place Jan. 23 and the other two within two or three days. Correspondents were told that at least 75 people were dragged out of the Pentecostal Unity Church, an adobe building in Campanario, a hamlet 24 miles east of the capital in San Vicente province. All 75 were killed by the troops, even though, the guerrillas said, the people in the church had no connection with rebels. The Americans were told that another 13 people were killed in the hamlet of Lomas de Angulo, about a quarter mile north of Campanario in the second attack, on or about Jan. 25. Salvadorans in the hamlet of San Benito, one mile south of Campanario, said another 15 peasants were killed by troops Jan. 23, including seven children and five adults. The villagers were not clear on the exact date of the Campanario massacre. Army troops were in the area Jan. 23 and again about two days later, and the killings occurred on one of those dates, they said. They said there was no fighting between soldiers and guerrillas either before or after the massacre. 'They put them into a column in front of the church and beheaded them,' one man said. Asked why the people were killed, the peasant said, 'for the crime of being poor.'"

Barbara Crossette of the *New York Times* reported the massacres in the following way on March 7: "Guerrillas and villagers in San Vicente Province say that Government security forces murdered a total of 124 people in this Salvadoran hamlet and two nearby hamlets in January, but the charges could not be verified on a visit to El Campanario today. Facts were hard to ascertain here, and there was evidence only of tragedy: 14 human skulls, blood-stained clothes, including a little girl's yellow dress, and several female scalps with thick black hair, one still adorned with an ornamental comb. . . . A guerrilla who identified himself only as Ephraim . . . said that a man who escaped the attack had told the rebels that about 30 soldiers had been responsible. He said they used machetes to kill the local people because the weapons were silent. He said that gunfire would have sounded a general alarm to the rebels. Tomás Escóbar, a 56-year-old peasant from nearby Las Lombras, and one of the few people seen along the hike into the reported massacre site, said that he thought that about 60 military men had been involved in the attack. When asked what uniforms they wore, he said 'all of them—the national police, the army, the national guard and some in civilian clothes.' He said that there seemed to be no motive for the reported killings. The guerrilla said that insurgent forces who found the bodies at the end of January informed Radio Venceremos, the rebel station, of the discovery. He did not say what use the rebel radio had made of the report."

On March 8, Dial Torgerson wrote again about the incidents in the *Los Angeles Times:* "In this area, a triangle with about 10-mile sides between the villages of Zacatecoluca and Tecoluca and the coastal road, El Salvador's army can advance only in great strength. And visible evidence here indicates that destruction was left behind in its last advance. Perhaps half the houses have been burned and lie in ruins. Many of the others have been abandoned. In one brick-walled farm house with a tile roof, two large bloodstains and a set of dentures mark the place where, neighbors said, a woman and her child were hacked to death with machetes by soldiers, who dumped their bodies into the back-yard well. Bones may be seen deep in the well."

Joanne Omang's March 8 report was printed by the *Washington Post* the next day: "The skulls were scattered down the gully behind the building like broken soccer balls. Counting the one in the wood storage pit, the one with spine and ribs that one guerrilla brought over on a stick, and the three in the blasted cornfield, and guessing at the larger fragments, there were 14 skulls in all. Trousers, shirts, dresses stained dark lay trampled in the dust yesterday in the village of El Campanario. . . . But the Salvadoran Government today insisted that the bones are those of the guerrillas' own war dead, saved just to be shown to foreign jounalists as part of a coordinated guerrilla effort to get U.S. aid to El Salvador cut off. . . . Asked why there were not more bones, more clothes, more skulls, [guerrillas] Nelson and Belisario shrugged. 'There were a lot more but the dogs carried them off,' Nelson said. 'After all, it's been two months.' Asked why they had waited so long to make this public, Nelson said it had been announced by guerrillas radio 'a few times' but that no one had paid much attention to it."

The *New York Times* printed Barbara Crossette's next report from San Salvador on March 9: "Fighting, which began before dawn, was reported by the Salvadoran armed forces to be widespread in San Vicente and San Miguel in the central and eastern parts of the country. . . . Here in the capital, the Salvadoran Army today responded to charges that it had been involved in the killing of peasants in three hamlets in San Vicente Province. Col. Marco Aurelio González, the army spokesman, said in an interview that the charges of a massacre had all the hallmarks of a guerrilla propaganda offensive. The spokesman acknowledged that there had been army operations in that area at the end of January but was unable to give details. . . . Sunday, a guerrilla in El Campanario at the site of one of the three areas where the killings were said to have taken place told reporters that the attackers had been members of the Atlacatl Battalion, the army's elite combat unit."

On March 13, the *Los Angeles Times* reported, "The Human Rights Commission of El Salvador said Friday that government forces killed 300 people in a January raid in San Vicente province, east of this capital city. Earlier, the commission had reported 100 dead in the raid, but a spokesman said that figure was revised upward after testimony from survivors and witnesses was fully reviewed. The government refuses to comment on reports by the commission—an independent group of priests, lawyers and other professionals—because authorities accuse it of being sympathetic to guerrillas fighting to overthrow the regime. The commission said the 300 people were killed during a military sweep Jan. 18–20 in five rural villages. The report lists the names of 59 of the people the commission said were killed. . . . Meanwhile, in Washington, two Democratic senators said they will try to give Congress a greater voice in any U.S. decision to engage in covert action in Central America or to send troops there. Sens. Paul Tsongas (D-Mass.) and Christopher J. Dodd (D-Conn.) said their initiative is prompted by concern about U.S. commitments in El Salvador and reported plans for covert action to destabilize Nicaragua."

CHAPTER
36

By the time the Salva- doran government's national elections were held on March 28, 1982, María's father was dead, his body bared to the waist to show mourners the wounds on his face and chest. María's mother had moved with her children to the house on the north-south highway at the edge of San Vicente, a shack already occupied by Felipe's parents, his sisters, and their children. Surrounding them were countless make-shift shacks filled with refugees from the volcano. On the day of the elections, María's mother went with her in-laws to the polling place in San Vicente. According to María, it was generally assumed that if people did not go to vote they were ready targets for local death squads. While the adults were gone, María and her brothers and cousins crouched before a thick wall of their house to avoid the bullets fired by government and FMLN soldiers outside the door.

Joanne Omang submitted a report from San Vicente to the *Washington Post* on March 28, printed the following day: "Gunfire rattled in the distance as heaving, jostling lines of people stretched from the single door of the San Vicente Community Center both ways around the block, and soft-drink sellers pushed their wares to the sweaty crowd intent on getting inside to cast their ballots. . . . In San Vicente and in many other cities, there was almost too much voting, and despite the almost total lack of transportation from the countryside into cities, people found ways to get to the polls. . . . Guerrillas have been urging people to cast blank ballots as indicators of support for the left, which is boycotting the elections as a farce. Guerrilla efforts to shut down all public transportation appeared to have been almost totally successful everywhere, however, leaving the roads eerily empty except for a few large trucks hauling voters, Red Cross vehicles carrying international observers and vans, taxis and cars full of journalists. By midafternoon, each of the 25 voting tables in the community center in San Vicente had counted 250 to 280 voters and the lines had vanished. 'People voted in the morning to get home before dark,' explained Victoria Galixto de Velasco, president of the provincial electoral board."

On the same day Richard J. Meislin reported on the polling process in Zacatecoluca to the *New York Times:* "The dusty roads outside this country's major eastern cities were awash with hundreds of people, walking and walking—sometimes for miles—to cast their ballots. On both sides of the Pan American Highway near Ilopango, east of San Salvador, a parade of people marched past ramshackle shanties and the billboards saying 'Your vote—the solution.' There were people young and old—men with canes, women carrying babies and women expecting them. Their attire of vivid yellows and greens and reds and magentas gave the impression of a traveling rainbow as they surged on foot along the scorching highway toward voting places in eastern El Salvador."

Zacatecoluca was the polling place where María's sister Marta would have voted. She herself was pregnant at the time. The baby died a few months after birth. It was the second child Marta had lost to malnutrition. By that time Marta was a widow; her husband's body and the bodies of three other coffee workers had been found decapitated in a ravine on the San Vicente volcano.

On April 23, Raymond Bonner reported from San Salvador for the *New York Times*, "Seven bodies were encountered on the road near Ilopango, on the eastern edge of the city. Four had been decapitated. It is clear from these and other findings that the killing goes on despite hopes that the March 28 elections for a constituent assembly would be the beginning of a nonviolent, democratic solution to the killings. . . . A worker at the Human Rights Commission said that before the elections they would find 20 to 25 bodies a week strewn around the perimeter of the capital. The number has risen to about 35 a week since the elections, he said."

According to a June 2 AP wire report printed the next day in the *New York Times*, "State department officials said today that the number of civilians being killed in El Salvador's civil war had shown a 'slight decline' since the March elections, down to about 250 a month."

"Some U.S. advisors in El Salvador are violating U.S. non-combat guidelines by 'fighting side by side' with government troops battling leftist rebels, CBS News said Wednesday night," reported the *Los Angeles Times* on June 24. "The network quoted unidentified Salvadoran soldiers as saying that on Tuesday advisers 'were firing 81-millimeter mortars against a rebel base' near a government camp along the Lempa River, about 45 miles southeast of San Salvador. . . . Last February, U.S. authorities relieved a U.S. lieutenant colonel of his duties in El Salvador and reprimanded six other advisers after Cable News Network filmed some of them carrying M-16 rifles."

Curt Suplee of the *Washington Post* wrote on June 15 that

"the current edition of the *American Poetry Review* contains an open letter signed by 146 poets including Pulitzer Prize winners Robert Penn Warren, John Ashbery, Maxine Kumin, Richard Wilbur, Stanley Kunitz, Richard Eberhart and Alan Dugan—protesting American aid to the government of El Salvador."

On July 3, John Dinges submitted this report to the *Washington Post:* "The International Committee of the Red Cross has 'made it clear that it is prepared to pull out of El Salvador because of growing concern over the Salvadoran armed forces' practice of not taking prisoners in battle,' according to a confidential State Department cable to the U.S. Embassy here. A member of the Red Cross delegation here, Andreas Balmer . . . said that virtually all of the approximately 550 political prisoners held by the Salvadoran government were arrested in noncombat situations and that there never have been more than a few captured on the battlefield during the country's 18-month civil war."

"Four American Catholic activists attempted to stage a hunger strike Wednesday in the well-protected U.S. Embassy to protest U.S. involvement with the Salvadoran regime," wrote Dial Torgerson on July 8 in the *Los Angeles Times*. "The attempt failed. Embassy officials gently eased the band of protesters out past the sandbags and shotguns and back onto the streets of San Salvador. . . . The four prayed first in the inner lobby of the embassy, which is known to staffers as 'Fort Apache,' as armed members of the U.S. Marine guard looked on curiously. A political officer rescinded an offer to let them remain, and they were ushered to the outer lobby, which faces a Marine and a receptionist through bullet-proof glass."

El Diario de Hoy reported on August 21, "According to military sources, joint forces of the 5th Infantry Brigade, Military Detachment No. 2 and the Atlacatl Battalion, supported by the Salvadoran Air Force, yesterday continued to search out and destroy terrorist camps in a large section of San Vicente. These actions began early this week with a classic 'pincers movement' in order to then carry out a 'hammer and anvil' operation. This operation, which is called Lt. Co. Mario Azenón Palma,' is being carried out on the slopes of the San Vicente volcano and in the area that covers Santa Clara, Santo Domingo, San Esteban Catarina, San Sebastian, San Pedro, San Felipe, and their cantons and villages. So far, it has been reported that the joint forces have destroyed several camps and have killed many guerrillas."

It must have been during this time, the summer and fall of 1982, that María, her mother, and her brothers went frequently to El Chile to work in the coffee fields, traveling by the more circuitous northern route around the volcano. The only paved road that led in this direction from San Vicente to El Chile went directly through towns and villages held at the time by the FMLN. The army's "hammer and anvil" operation, following its "pincers movement," was surely the campaign witnessed by María as it progressed on land and in the air through the FMLN-held areas and up toward El Chile and the surrounding hamlets on Chinchontepec's western slope.

On August 30, *Diario Latino* reported: "After carrying out a second stage of the cleanup and control operation in southeastern San Vincente, the Ramón Belloso, Atlacatl and other military units regrouped in their garrisons. Many casualties were inflicted on the guerrillas in the area covering San Vicente, surrounding the Lempa River and Chinchontepec, because the army covered Tecoluca and the region where the Injiboa (sugar mill) operates. The military operation involved approximately 4,000 men and comprised more than 40 percent of San Vicente Department and part of La Paz Department."

"Three peasant women charge that Salvadoran government troops used fighter-bombers, grenades and automatic
weapons to massacre 300 unarmed villagers during a recent
drive against leftist guerrillas," the *Los Angeles Times* reported
on September 8. "The government denies the assertions
made during a news conference Monday by the Salvadoran
Human Rights Commission, which is generally considered to
be careful about confirming such charges. The women said
that U.S.-built A-37 fighter-bombers, incendiary bombs,
hand grenades and automatic weapons were used to wipe out
peasants who had been driven by government forces into a
section of San Vicente province, an area east of the capital of
San Salvador, which is dominated by leftist guerrillas. The
women, who requested anonymity, said that the victims were
mostly guerrilla supporters living in the hamlet of Amatitan
Arriba, about 45 miles east of San Salvador. They said no
armed insurgents were present when the alleged attacks began Aug. 18. 'The people tried to leave through the valleys
and they cornered them. They killed a mountain of people—
children, old people and women,' one woman said. . . . A
government military spokesman, asked about the news conference, said Tuesday that it is a common rebel tactic to claim
that guerrillas killed were civilians. 'This is misinformation,'
he said. The woman said peasants from a 40-square-mile area
under rebel control had fled into Amatitan Arriba as troops
encircled their villages in mid-August. 'Many people threw
themselves off cliffs to escape the fire,' one woman said. 'The
families that were there spent seven days without eating or
sleeping. . . . At night they bombed with lights so they could
see the people and where they saw them they shot them. The
fighting lasted seven days. Since no one answered their fire,
the soldiers were persecuting us. They hunted us like animals.' Dozens of people escaped, traveling by foot to San Salvador, she said."

Havana International Service reported on the same day that "the Salvadoran Army murdered 300 elderly persons, women and children during a military operation on 18 August in San Vicente Department in which napalm bombs were used. . . . The survivors said that after the bombing, in which large areas of land were scorched, the troops of the genocidal regime swept through the region with grenades and automatic weapons, indiscriminately killing unarmed children, women and elderly persons."

On September 13, *Radio Cadena YSKL* broadcast a news conference by Salvadoran Defense Minister Gen. José Guillermo García at the Armed Forces Press Committee office in San Salvador. FBIS published the translation of the live broadcast on September 14:

Q: General, do you think that the training that some of the troops have received in the United States has had an important effect on the troops' efficiency and how could we, as journalists, note that improvement?

A: Of course, I can say with pleasure that we have seen a definite improvement. Moreover, it is indisputable that any kind of special training like that which our people received in the United States should produce differences. Of course, we have noted this in the results of the operations that have been carried out recently. Worthy of note, for example, was the operation in San Vicente. For the first time, no one was killed. You remember that the ambush was not a part of this military operation that was under way in San Vicente, the ambush occurred far from the area in which the operation was taking place. However, with great satisfaction, I can tell you that during this military operation, for the first time we did not have a single death. This speaks well of the level of training and for the competence of our people as a result of this training. Of course, you will have heard, you know from what source, that there were 1,000 or 1,500 deaths. However, all the Salvadoran people know that this is just the propaganda that is heard over and over again. That is all.

Q: At the end of the last military offensive operation in San Vicente, exactly how many guerrilla casualties were there?

A: If I am not mistaken, there were approximately 54 casualties in the northern part and approximately 223 or 225 in the southern part. In total it is the result we have mentioned, as far as the amount is concerned.

Q: Some local stations say women, children and elderly people died among the guerrillas casualties reported by the armed forces. What is your opinion?

A: That is part of the scheme of confusion they are setting up to influence public opinion. But in all honesty, I want to tell you that we have tried to investigate this and the results have been completely negative. Of course, I don't wish, at this time, to deny that on some occasions innocent people may have died in some action. I am not going to deny this. But it has taken place sporadically and in other places, and not as they try to portray it, disregarding what really happened.

Q: Then you (words indistinct, FBIS) were by accident or wounds, how many civilians died during this operation?

A: I could not tell you. But I do want to tell you that some people have died, maybe people who had nothing to do with the problem. But we refer back to your first question regarding how to determine who is a guerrilla and who is not. It is very difficult to make that judgment.

Q: General, about one week ago some reporters tried to go to Amatitan Arriba canton where peasants and a civil

defense commander denounced the death of several unarmed persons, possibly most of them guerrilla supporters. They could not go in because the troops stationed
there did not let us go beyond the town of Santa Clara.
May I ask: Is it possible for some reporters to go there to
see how the place was left?

A: I believe that if there was no permission for you to go into
the place you were so interested in, it was due purely to
combat reasons, so that you must understand that cir-
cumstances so demand. Please be sure that as soon as
there is a chance for you to go, you may do so, if you are
so interested. Be sure that you may tell the world the
truth, that you may tell exactly what happened there.
Your interest also speaks about the interest you might
have in telling the truth. Please be sure that we have no
objections whatsoever to lending you the facilities to make
your analyses and tell the world the truth."

A *Managua Radio Sandino* broadcast on October 6, according to FBIS, reported, "U.S. Lt. Col. John Buchanan told
SALPRESS in an interview that despite the massive U.S. military aid and U.S. training of Salvadoran soldiers, the military
situation in El Salvador has reached a stalemate. According to
Buchanan, a U.S. adviser admitted to him that 9 of the regime's 13 major military leaders are pathological criminals,
alcoholics and rapists. He also said that the U.S. advisers
would like to get rid of them but that this would amount to
disintegration of the already exhausted Salvadoran military
system."

On November 5, the *New York Times* printed the following
report by Bernard Weinraub from San Salvador: "The Unites
States Ambassador to El Salvador, describing the Salvadoran
legal system as 'rotten,' has threatened an end to military aid

unless human rights 'abuses' by the security forces here are stopped. . . . The Ambassador told about 450 businessmen that the rightist 'mafia' that kidnapped and murdered political opponents here posed as much of a threat to El Salvador as leftist guerrillas. The speech startled many of the businessmen—members of the American Chamber of Commerce—and about a dozen of them walked out. The Chamber of Commerce—which represents some of the most powerful business interests in El Salvador, attacked Mr. Hinton today in a full-page advertisement in a morning newspaper, *El Diario de Hoy*."

The next day Weinraub wrote in the *New York Times:* "Salvador's Defense Minister said today that he agreed with American criticism of the nation's legal system, but said it was 'unfair' of the American Ambassador to maintain that as many as 30,000 Salvadorans had been murdered in the last three years. . . . 'I told Hinton that I didn't agree with the part of the speech where he mentions 30,000 murders,' said General García in Spanish. 'It's the wrong figure. It's an unfair figure.' Asked for the correct figure, General García replied, 'I can't say.'"

On November 10, the *New York Times* printed another report by Weinraub: "Administration officials said today that the United States Ambassador to El Salvador had been told to refrain from making public criticisms of human rights abuses by Salvadoran security forces."

On December 4, Philip Taubman reported for the *New York Times* that "United States covert activities in Central America, which began a year ago with limited aims, have become the most ambitious paramilitary and political action operation mounted by the Central Intelligence Agency in nearly a decade, according to intelligence officials. . . . The Central American operations have caused growing concern in Congress, the Defense Department and the State Department. Some officials fear . . . that the efforts of the C.I.A. are dependent on extremist groups it cannot control."

On December 22, *Havana International Service* reported that "according to the military high command, a new antiguerrilla operation with approximately 1,000 troops participating has been launched in San Vicente Department."

On December 31, *Havana International Service* reported, "The Salvadoran Air Force has continued its intense bombing of presumed guerrilla positions in the vicinity of the Chinchontepec volcano in San Vicente Department."

Panama City ACAN reported on January 15, 1983: "A total of 5,840 civilians were murdered in El Salvador during 1982, or an average of 16 per day. This adds up to 36,000 persons killed for political reasons during the last 4 years. According to the Salvadoran Human Rights Commission, an unofficial organization, 1,663 of the almost 6,000 political murders of 1982 were peasants and 3,577 victims were never identified. The months with the greatest number of political murders were March and May, with 905 and 868, respectively. The months with the fewest murders were July and September, with 132 and 143, respectively, said the commission. The commission reported that 1,084 people were reported arrested and missing. However, the commission said that another 4,000 persons disappeared but were not openly reported because relatives of the victims feared reprisals."

By this time María's mother was already dead. Her eldest daughter Marta stayed with her in-laws and her only surviving child in El Chile. In San Vicente, Cándida's four youngest children went into the streets.

CHAPTER

37

It was the afternoon of my seventh day in the newspaper and periodical room of the Library of Congress annex on Independence Avenue. After I put away the last reel of microfilm, I went out into the basement corridor to the pay telephones and made a long-distance call to my mother's house. "María," I said excitedly when she had got on the line, "you've told me that your mother's picture was in the newspaper after she died. I've been looking at many newspaper pictures of El Salvador, and I have a feeling that the photograph could be in one of two papers I've seen. There were lots of pictures in both of them."

I saw in my mind once more the thousands of black-and-white identification photographs of missing and suspected dead persons printed in the newspapers. Photograph after photograph of young men and women in their teens and twenties appeared on the newspaper pages above captions in bold letters that read "DESAPARECIÓ," or simply "ASESINADA." I saw again the thousands of black-and-white news photos of mutilated bodies accompanying announcements of anonymous killings. It was the unique characteristic of this brutal social order that newspapers "freely" displayed the evidence of right-wing terror on their pages. Against these pictorial scenes of brutality, as on the streets, the eye experienced no censorship. Only the mind was not allowed to reflect on the identities of the perpetrators, nor on their connections or whereabouts. Those concerns were given no room in the newspapers. They remained invisible, silent.

María had told me that the picture of her mother in the newspaper was taken "before she died—she looked so pretty."

"María, I think that together you and I might be able to find the newspaper picture of your mother," I said. "It might take a while, but I think we can do it. What do you say? Would you like me to come and get you so that we can return here and look for the picture together?"

I heard María gasp on the other end of the line. After a distinct pause, I heard the familiar sound of her breathing, and I knew that she had heaved a big sigh and broken into a smile.

Three days later, María and I walked into the Library of Congress newspaper and periodical room. She had dressed up for the occasion, wearing the turquoise corduroy jumper my mother had made for her and patent leather shoes. I filled out the request slips for the newspapers I needed, and in less than fifteen minutes the first reels of microfilm were brought in on a cart.

María sat straight as a board on the chair and observed every detail as I showed her how to use the viewing machine. As always, her bearing suggested that she was totally prepared, entirely collected. I put in the first reel. Local news and photographs of citizens tended to come on page 4 or 5, after the international news and the military and political news on the national pages. Slowly, María turned the lever as page after page of headlines, political news, military updates,

I.D. photos of missing persons, soccer news, furniture adver-
tisements, and beauty queen contestants glided by.

The hand lever creaked and the film made its familiar
scratching sound as it moved. We had been sitting in front of
the screen, scanning page after page, for almost two hours. I
tried to put out of my mind the thought that we could be sitting in front of the viewing machine like this for days, for
weeks—perhaps to no avail. What if María had made a mis-
take? What if the photograph was a dream? What were we
doing in Washington after all? Why was I spending my time
like this, looking for a newspaper photograph of my daughter's biological mother? And why put María through this
emotional torture? Enough people had told me to stop being
so obsessed about María's past, including my own mother.
"Why dig in old wounds?" she had said more than once. "Just
be a mother to the child."

We had finished with another set of classified pages, and
the screen showed new headlines, international and national
news, a tennis tournament and another soccer match thrown
in to alleviate the tedium of the war news, followed by the social page and a gala ball thrown by a businessmen's club. I
heard María's regular breathing as she looked carefully up
and down each page and turned the level with a confident,
steady hand. She was clearly intent upon her goal. If she
could hold out, why shouldn't I? I had to trust her faith in this
process.

Slowly María's hand turned the lever. Another date appeared on the screen. Again we watched the international
and national pages glide by. I heard the creaking of the lever,
heard María's breathing next to me. I rubbed the back of my
neck—it had become stiff from more than a week of looking
up at the screen. Then I noticed that the creaking had
stopped—María had taken her hand from the lever.

There were three photographs on the screen. My eye

moved quickly away from the photo closest to my view—five men in business suits holding a banner. Out of the corner of my eye I had already noticed that the remaining two photographs were snapshots of women. My eyes moved to the picture at the left of the page showing a mass of dark hair, the dark-light contrast dominating the picture. It was a pretty woman with warm eyes and a full mouth, with just the hint of a sweet smile—younger than I would have expected. I scanned the caption—"LA SEÑORITA RECIBE MEDALLA . . . 'promesa artística 1982.'" I read no more. I looked quickly over to María. She was staring at the third photograph. I knew from her eyes even before I looked at the photograph that this was the one.

I recognized immediately the wide heart-shaped face, coming, just like María's, to a delicate point at the chin. I recognized the faint frown, the piercing eyes looking aside toward the right, beyond the camera and its operator, as it were. I recognized the determined, pursed mouth. I recognized even the wisps of hair that insisted on framing the face even though the hair was pulled straight back in a bun. "SAN VICENTE—ACCIDENTE," read the caption. Stunned, I read no more, but stared at the woman in the picture. Here she was at last, face to face with me—María's mother.

María sat back in her seat. Slowly, she looked over to me. Her face was flushed. I will never forget the astonished look, the sadness and relief in her eyes.

"As a result of injuries suffered from a fall from a Ferris wheel at the San Vicente fairgrounds, Señora Cándida Remas Ramírez, age 38, died in the hospital," the text read in Spanish. A short article on the other side of the page explained that two other people had incurred minor injuries, and that relatives of the deceased went the next day to place a complaint before city officials.

"I know it is my mother, but I don't remember her so

much like this," ventured María. "I think I remember her better in my heart. She look there more soft and happy like I really remember her."

"I think she was angry when the picture was taken," I said. "The picture is from her identification card. The cédula—that's how the military keeps track of the people. She had a right to be angry, because she was forced to have her I.D. picture taken, and forced to carry her cédula with her all the time. So in the picture, her face showed how she felt."

"I know, my mother have to show the piece of paper to the Guardias every time we go to the market," María said. "If somebody doesn't have the paper with the picture and the numbers, they shoot."

"Yes," I said.

"Anyway, I'm glad I can see the picture of my mother," María said at last with a deep sigh. "Remember, I tell you a long time ago, my mother's picture was in the newspaper. I think you didn't believe me. But now, see, it is true. Now I can remember my mother in my heart, and I can see the picture, too."

We stood up from our chairs and went to the coin-operated machine across the room to make copies of the page with the picture of María's mother. Then we left the annex and crossed Independence Avenue to the main building of the Library of Congress. There we ordered a negative, which the Library of Congress would prepare for us from the microfilm for a small fee. I filled out the request slip while María sat on a bench and scrutinized for herself the photocopied newsprint page with the picture of her mother.

After we found Mar-
ía's mother's picture,
we went to a Salva-
doran restaurant in
the Adams-Morgan district
of Washington to celebrate.
Even before we scanned the
entire menu, we ordered María's favorite, which was *pupusas,* thick Salvadoran corn
tortillas filled with cheese and
meat, eaten with a garnish of
shredded carrots, cabbage,
and chili peppers. Then we
looked around at the colorful
posters of El Salvador on the
walls, listened to the taped
Salvadoran music, chatted
with people at the neighboring tables. We relished the
pupusas, followed by tamales
and salads, several glasses of a
tamarindo drink, and finally,
strong black coffee—
into which, for her
cup, María poured
three heaping tea-
spoons of sugar. We skipped
dessert.

Swish, swish, scrape,
scrape—somebody was sweeping on the other side of the
small door behind me. Swish,
swish, scrape, scrape—I remembered the sounds, the
men in dark brown uni-
forms at the Hotel Presidente
sweeping near the cabanas. I
remembered the wrinkled,
leathery face of the man who
stopped to look over and
smile at me. Now the sweeping had stopped, and I heard
someone open and close a
cabinet. María and I both
turned as the small door be-

hind me was opened from the other side and a young man in a black waiter's uniform—or rather a boy, he couldn't have been older than fifteen—came through the doorway. He nodded a greeting to the waiter who had been serving our area of the restaurant and began clearing the table next to us.

It was as if I recognized him from somewhere. His arms, hands, and fingers moved in perfect unison, quickly and skillfully gathering up the remaining plates, cups, saucers, flatware, and piling them in a steady heap on the tray. He lifted the vase of flowers and the salt and pepper shakers and ashtray to remove any last crumbs from the tablecloth. He swiftly laid new place settings—and in less than a minute the table had been cleared, cleaned off, and reset. The boy moved pantherlike between the restaurant and the kitchen, his joints and limbs as if in flight, his feet seeming hardly to touch the ground. All this in silence. In the busy restaurant filled with loud, laughing Salvadorans, he had not yet said a word. No one from the city could have such quiet balance and self-assurance. It was clear that he was from the countryside.

For just a moment I noticed him glance sideways at María. She had lowered her head but was still watching him. There was an uncanny resemblance between them: he had the same smooth dark brown skin, the smooth hair, the same wide face and dark almond eyes. Now I saw that of all the Salvadorans in the room, only this boy and María looked as though they had far more Indian than Spanish blood.

"Mamá!" María whispered excitedly, and I turned and saw that her face was flushed for the second time that day. "He look just like my brother Miguel!"

When he came to our table to offer us more coffee—the expression on his face neither serious nor smiling—I tried to begin a conversation, to ask him where in El Salvador he might be from.

"Mamá!" Her face beet-red, María looked at me imploringly, then quickly squeezed my hand under the table so that it hurt. "Don't you see, he doesn't speak English!" she whispered hoarsely under her breath.

The boy turned and went away before I could formulate a question in Spanish. Anyway, I reconsidered because María was chiding me. "Mamá!" she continued in her hoarse whisper. "Don't you know it's impolite to ask somebody questions like that if they're not ready. Don't you know, in Salvador strangers don't talk like that to each other, especially if one is a boy and the other is a girl—or a woman. Mamá, you don't know anything! Maybe it's dangerous and he doesn't want to talk about himself!"

Before I could respond, or even think about what I would want to say, the boy returned to our table with a bag of pupusas which we had ordered to take home with us. As he set the bag on the table he turned toward María and asked quietly, "De Salvador?"

Her eyes told him yes, that was where she was from.

"¿La madre?" he asked, gesturing toward me.

María and I both smiled. "Adoptiva," I said with a slight hesitation, looking quickly at María to check if she would approve of this. She didn't seem to mind.

"Ah, adoptiva. ¿De donde es la niña?" he asked me.

I looked over at María—she was waiting for me to respond. "De San Vicente," I answered. "Del volcán Chinchontepec."

"Ah, sí, comprendo. Comprendo." And he smiled.

"¿Y usted?" I asked him. "¿De donde es usted?"

"Soy de Usulután," he answered. That was the neighboring province to the east of San Vicente. María's father and uncles had sometimes gone there by truck to the Lempa River and brought home fish to eat.

"Ah, de Usulután," I said, and asked him if his family was still there.

He smiled—he obviously didn't want to talk about his family. But after a pause, he said he had a younger sister. "Como la niña," he said, nodding to María. "¿Cuántos años tienes?" he asked her.

"Ocho," she responded faintly, her face again flushed.

"Ah, ocho años," he said with a smile, and for a few moments his eyes rested on hers. Then, as if waking from a dream, he caught himself and stepped back from the table, told us he hoped we would enjoy the pupusas, and walked away.

"He look so much like Miguel!" said María once again, quite dazed, after he was gone. We sat at the table in silence for a while. I thought of María's descriptions of her family. "Miguel and Ramón and I have softer, smoother hair, more like our mother. Marta and Aurelio have the hair more rough, more like our father."

My mind's eye held the face of the boy again, the gestures, the expression. Then I remembered. It was as though I had seen him once before. He looked exactly like one of the boys at the boys' orphanage where we had picked up Aurelio, one of the adolescent boys leaning awkwardly, tentatively, against the orphanage wall. It had been the moment I first understood that we were the ones who would never forget.

"Someday, I promise you, María," I said suddenly, stunned by my own words. "I promise you, someday we'll find out exactly what has happened to your brother and sister."

The next day we de-cided that enough was enough. We drafted a letter to Miguel and Marta. We said, María de Jesús is fine, you don't need to worry. She has been adopted and she is all right. Aurelio and Ramón are safe and well, too. We would like to find you and help; we hope you are some-where. If you want to get in touch with María de Jesús and her new mother, this is how.

Then we sent the letter, translated by friends into Spanish, via the underground railroad, southward, back to the red-brown-green mountains of El Salvador.

OUR NEW HAMMOCK

Several times a day
our city police helicopter
chops away at the wind,
zigzags above our neighborhood
looking for stolen cars,
abandoned souls,
forbidden exchanges
in back lots and spring gardens.

It is sundown. María stands in the yard
rocking her dolls in our new hammock;
carefully she arranges leg next to leg,
arm to arm, cheek to cheek.
"This is how our mother in Salvador
put us to sleep in the hammock
except we were hanging over the bed
and when she was lying down giving
her milk to the baby
she gave us a push like this with her leg."

Cándida. Can you still hear the whine
of the bombers, the murders, the cries?
Or have you tried your strong, reliable arms,
your legs (I know them well from your daughter's),
pushed your way out of the box and crawled
sweating, in a bloodstained orange dress
toward El Norte;
tunneled beneath borders, undermined checkpoints,
kneading the earth with your hands,
grinding it into meal with your teeth
till you've reached the evening of our back yard
and rested your head, under our new hammock?

Cándida. Give María another push with your leg
as she swings with her doll babies into the wind.

Helen Hooven Santmyer Prize Winners

This Strange Society of Women
Reading the Letters and Lives of the Woman's Commonwealth

Sally L. Kitch

Making Stories, Making Selves
Feminist Reflections on the Holocaust

R. Ruth Linden